HOLY BIBLE
Divine
PRAYERS

The Perfect Prayers

A Path to Spiritual Fulfillment

Bema D Yeo

Copyright Notice

Disclaimer

The information provided in "The Perfect Prayers: A Path to Spiritual Fulfillment" is intended for general knowledge and spiritual growth. The author, Bema D Yeo, does not assume any responsibility or liability for any actions taken based on the content of this book. The prayers and guidance provided are meant to support personal reflection and spiritual practice but are not a substitute for professional advice or counseling. Individual experiences may vary, and readers are encouraged to seek appropriate guidance tailored to their personal needs. Any reliance on the information in this book is at the reader's own risk.

Divine Prayers

I wrote "The Perfect Prayers: A Path to Spiritual Fulfillment" to share the prayers from my personal journey of spiritual discovery and to offer the wisdom I found along the way. Throughout my own quest for enlightenment, I encountered moments of profound peace and clarity, which I captured in these prayers. I believe everyone deserves to find inner peace, and this book provides the tools to achieve it. Each prayer is crafted to offer guidance and solace in times of joy and challenge, helping readers navigate their spiritual paths with greater ease and confidence. By sharing these prayers, I hope to inspire others to explore their spirituality and deepen their connection with the divine.

I firmly believe that everyone deserves to find inner peace, and "The Perfect Prayers" is designed to offer the tools needed to achieve it. Life is filled with both joyful and challenging moments, and having a spiritual anchor can make a significant difference in how we navigate these experiences. The prayers in this book offer guidance and solace, acting as a source of comfort and strength. Whether you are celebrating a triumph or facing a difficult time, these prayers are here to help you find balance and serenity. They *encourage self-reflection and introspection, fostering personal growth and enlightenment.*

Furthermore, my hope is that this book will inspire others to explore their spirituality and deepen their connection with the divine. It is not just about individual growth but also about building a community of like-minded individuals who support and uplift each other in their spiritual pursuits. By empowering readers to take control of their spiritual development, "The Perfect Prayers" aims to create a ripple effect of positive change. Together, we can build a network of support, sharing in the collective quest for spiritual fulfillment and inner peace. This book is an invitation to join this journey and find the divine connection that resides within us all.

Divine Prayers
www.divineprayers.org

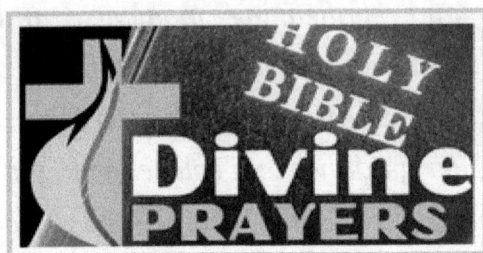

To all those who seek solace in prayer, whose hearts are open to the whispers of the divine, and whose souls are touched by the timeless beauty of spiritual communion. May this book serve as a guiding light on your journey of faith, offering comfort, wisdom, and inspiration as you navigate the sacred path of prayer.

Prologue

In the vast journey of life, we often seek moments of stillness, clarity, and connection. "The Perfect Prayers: A Path to Spiritual Fulfillment" is born from this universal longing. It is a collection of prayers that serve as both a beacon and a bridge, guiding us towards a deeper understanding of ourselves and our place in the cosmos. It is within this hallowed silence that prayers are whispered with faith, their words transcending the boundaries of the physical realm to touch the very heart of the universe.

For centuries, across cultures and continents, prayers have been woven into the fabric of human existence, serving as beacons of hope, solace, and guidance in times of joy and sorrow alike. Each prayer in this book has been crafted with the intention of bringing solace, strength, and enlightenment to its reader. Whether you are in a moment of joy or facing challenges, these prayers are meant to be a companion, offering words of wisdom and comfort. They are not confined by any single tradition but draw from the essence of universal spiritual truths, making them accessible to all who seek a richer, more meaningful spiritual life.

"The Perfect Prayers" is an exploration of this timeless tradition–a journey into the depths of the soul, where the mundane meets the sacred, and the finite touches the infinite. Within these pages lie treasures of wisdom, insight, and inspiration, drawn from the collective wisdom of sages, saints, and seekers throughout history. It is a testament to the enduring power of prayer to uplift, transform, and illuminate the human experience.

As we embark on this odyssey of the spirit, may we open our hearts to the beauty of divine communion, and may the prayers contained herein be a source of comfort, strength, and enlightenment on our journey toward the divine. Through "The Perfect Prayers," may you find the peace and fulfillment that you seek. Let these words resonate in your heart, illuminate your path, and bring you closer to the divine essence that resides within and around us all.

Table of Contents

Prayers to Fighting Fear

The Devil's Use of Fear- The devil and his agents frequently utilize fear as a potent weapon to manipulate and control individuals. Fear has the power to distort perceptions, impair judgment, and paralyze actions, making it an effective tool for spiritual warfare. By instilling fear, the devil seeks to sow doubt, confusion, and hopelessness in people's hearts and minds. This tactic can undermine faith, disrupt relationships, and create a sense of isolation, thereby hindering spiritual growth and progress. Fear can also divert individuals from their God-given purposes, causing them to focus more on potential dangers than on divine promises and guidance.

The devil employs various mechanisms to instill fear, including lies, deception, and intimidation. He may magnify potential threats, exaggerate consequences, or create imaginary dangers to exploit your vulnerabilities. By playing on insecurities and uncertainties, the devil can amplify anxiety and stress, leading people to question your abilities and worth. This fear can manifest in different forms, such as fear of failure, rejection, or the unknown. These fears can become so overwhelming that they can prevent you from stepping out in faith, taking risks, or pursuing their God-given dreams.

How fear impacts our lives and the importance of fighting fear - Fear directly impacts faith by eroding trust in God's promises and His character. When individuals are consumed by fear, they may struggle to believe that God is in control and that He has their best interests at heart. This lack of trust can lead to spiritual stagnation and a weakened relationship with God. Fighting fear is crucial for maintaining spiritual health and fulfilling one's purpose. Overcoming fear allows individuals to walk in the freedom and confidence that comes from knowing and trusting God. It enables them to face challenges with courage, embrace new opportunities, and live out their faith authentically. By combating fear, individuals can break free from the enemy's control and live a life characterized by peace, joy, and purpose. The Bible provides clear guidance on this, as seen in Isaiah 41:10, which states,

"So do not fear, for I am with you; do not be dismayed, for I am your God". **Isaiah 41:10**

Prayer 1: Anchored in Faith

Dear Lord,

As it is written in Psalm 27:1, "The Lord is my light and my salvation; whom shall I fear?" Lord, I seek refuge in your presence to dispel fear.

I pray that my faith in you grows, and that I may find the courage needed to overcome all the fears that assail me. May your love cast out fear from my heart.

In Jesus' name, I pray, Amen.

Prayer 2: Trusting in His Peace

Dear Lord,

Your Word reminds us in John 14:27 that you leave us your peace, a peace that surpasses all understanding. Lord, I turn to you to combat the fear that overwhelms me.

I pray that your peace floods my heart, dispelling all anxiety. Allow me to find refuge in you, knowing that your peace is greater than fear.

In Jesus' name, I pray, Amen.

Prayer 3: Boldness through His Strength

Dear Lord,

Your Word assures us in Philippians 4:13 that "I can do all things through Christ who strengthens me." Lord, I acknowledge my weakness, but I find my strength in you.

I pray that you grant me the strength needed to resist fear and anxiety. Allow me to walk boldly, knowing that you strengthen me.

In Jesus' name, I pray, Amen.

Prayer 4: Conquer with His Perfect Love

Dear Lord,

Your Word teaches us in 1 John 4:18 that "There is no fear in love, but perfect love casts out fear." Lord, I pray that you fill my heart with love to drive out fear.

Allow me to live in confidence in your perfect love, knowing that nothing can separate me from you. May your love dispel every fear that dares to rise.

In Jesus' name, I pray, Amen.

Prayer 5: Strength in the Face of Fear

Dear Lord,

Your Word assures us in Isaiah 41:10, "Fear not, for I am with you; be not dismayed, for I am your God; I will strengthen you, I will help you, I will uphold you with my righteous right hand."

Lord, I pray that your strength supports me and your presence comforts me in times of fear. Allow me to find peace in knowing that you are by my side.

In Jesus' name, I pray, Amen.

Prayer 6: Strength in the Face of Fear

Dear Lord,

Your Word assures us in Isaiah 41:10, "Fear not, for I am with you; be not dismayed, for I am your God; I will strengthen you, I will help you, I will uphold you with my righteous right hand."

Lord, I pray that your strength supports me and your presence comforts me in times of fear. Allow me to find peace in knowing that you are by my side.

In Jesus' name, I pray, Amen.

Prayer 7: Fearless in His Presence

Dear Lord,

As it is written in Psalm 23:4, "Even though I walk through the valley of the shadow of death, I will fear no evil, for you are with me." Lord, I seek refuge in your presence to dispel fear.

I pray that your presence becomes my source of confidence and comfort. May I move forward without fear, knowing that you are by my side.

In Jesus' name, I pray, Amen.

Prayer 8: Guided by His Light

Dear Lord,

As it is written in Psalm 27:1, "The Lord is my light and my salvation; whom shall I fear?" Lord, I turn to you, the source of my strength and light.

Allow me to walk in the light of your presence, knowing that you are my salvation and stronghold. May your light dispel all darkness and guide me in moments of doubt and fear.

In Jesus' name, I pray, Amen.

Prayer 9: Fear Not, For I Am With You (Isaiah 41:10)

Almighty God, as I stand before the shadows of uncertainty and fear, I am reminded of Your words in Isaiah, "Fear not, for I am with you; Be not dismayed, for I am your God." In this moment of prayer, I seek the comfort of Your presence and the strength of Your promise.

Lord, You are my rock and my fortress. In the midst of turmoil, Your word in Psalm 23 assures me, "Even though I walk through the darkest valley, I will fear no evil, for you are with me." Grant me the courage to face my fears, knowing that You are by my side.

As David declared in Psalm 27, "The Lord is my light and my salvation–whom shall I fear?" I ask for Your light to guide me through darkness and Your salvation to lift the weight of fear from my heart. Replace my anxious thoughts with the peace that transcends all understanding, as promised in Philippians 4:6-7.

Help me to trust in You with all my heart, leaning not on my own understanding, as Proverbs 3:5-6 instructs. Strengthen my faith, that I may stand firm in the assurance of Your love and protection.

In the face of fear, I choose to cling to Your promises, for You are faithful and just. May Your grace and mercy follow me all the days of my life, as I dwell in the house of the Lord forever.

In Jesus' name, I pray

Amen.

Personal notes:

_____

_____

_____

_____

_____

_____

_____

_____

_____

_____

_____

_____

_____

_____

_____

_____

_____

Prayers for Depression

The devil and his agents often use depression as a powerful tool to attack and weaken you spiritually, emotionally, and physically. As stated in **John 10:10**, **"*The thief comes only to steal and kill and destroy; I have come that they may have life, and have it to the full*.**" This verse highlights the devil's intent to rob you of the abundant life that Jesus promises. Depression can lead to overwhelming feelings of worthlessness, hopelessness, and isolation, making it difficult to maintain your faith and trust in God's goodness. By amplifying negative thoughts and emotions, the devil seeks to ensnare you in a cycle of despair, preventing you from experiencing the joy, peace, and purpose that God intends for your life.

Overcoming Depression with Faith- To combat the devil's use of depression, it is crucial to rely on God's promises and seek His strength. **Psalm 34:18** reassures you, **"*The Lord is close to the brokenhearted and saves those who are crushed in spiri*t.**" This verse reminds you that God is near and attentive to your suffering, offering comfort and hope even in your darkest moments. By focusing on God's unwavering love and faithfulness, you can resist the lies and deceptions of the devil. Engaging in spiritual practices such as prayer, scripture reading, and worship can help you draw closer to God and find solace in His presence.

Prayer 1: Light in My Darkness (Psalm 18:28)

Lord, as I walk through this valley of depression, I am reminded of Your words in Psalm 18:28, "You light a lamp for me. The Lord, my God, lights up my darkness." In these challenging times, I ask for Your light to shine through the shadows of my heart.

Dispel the darkness with the brightness of Your hope and love. Grant me the strength to face each day, and the courage to seek joy in the smallest of blessings. Let Your presence be a constant reminder that I am never alone in this struggle.

In Jesus' name, I pray,

Amen.

Prayer 2: Cast My Cares (1 Peter 5:7)

Heavenly Father, in this moment of despair, I hold onto the promise of 1 Peter 5:7, "Cast all your anxiety on him because he cares for you." I lay before You all my burdens, my fears, and my worries.

Help me to trust in Your unfailing love and care. Replace the heaviness in my heart with Your peace. Guide me to find rest in Your comforting embrace, knowing that You are with me, caring for every aspect of my life.

In Jesus' name, I pray,

Amen.

Prayer 3: Renew My Strength (Isaiah 40:31)

Dear God, as I battle with depression, I draw inspiration from Isaiah 40:31, "But those who hope in the Lord will renew their strength." I pray for the renewal of my spirit and mind.

Lift me on the wings of Your hope. Rejuvenate my weary heart and fill me with the strength to overcome. Help me to see beyond my current circumstances, to a future filled with Your grace and promise.

In Jesus' name, I pray,

Amen.

Prayer 4: Hope and Renewal (Lamentations 3:22-23)

Dear God, in the depths of despair, I cling to the hope found in Lamentations 3:22-23, "The steadfast love of the Lord never ceases; His mercies never come to an end; they are new every morning." Each day, remind me of Your never-ending love and the promise of a new beginning.

Grant me the strength to face each morning with hope. Renew my spirit, Lord, and guide me on a path toward healing and peace. Let Your mercies light up my path and bring joy to my heart.

In Jesus' name, I pray,

Amen.

Prayer 5: Comfort in the Storm (Matthew 11:28)

Merciful Savior, in these moments of inner turmoil and despair, I remember Your invitation in Matthew 11:28, "Come to me, all who labor and are heavy laden, and I will give you rest." I come to You seeking rest and comfort.

Ease the burden of my heart and calm the storm within my soul. Help me to find rest in Your presence, and solace in Your loving embrace. Teach me to lay down my burdens at Your feet and find peace in Your care.

In Jesus' name, I pray, Amen.

Prayer 6: My Refuge and Strength (Psalm 46:1)

Heavenly Father, in the midst of my depression, I seek solace in Your word, remembering Psalm 46:1, "God is our refuge and strength, an ever-present help in trouble." Lord, be my refuge in these times of distress. Embrace me with Your strength and guide me through this darkness.

Fill my heart with Your unwavering love and remind me that You are always with me. Lift the weight of sadness from my shoulders and replace it with Your peace, which surpasses all understanding.

In Jesus' name, I pray,

Amen.

Prayer 7: Joy Comes in the Morning (Psalm 30:5)

Heavenly Father, in these moments of deep despair, I am reminded of the hope expressed in Psalm 30:5, "Weeping may tarry for the night, but joy comes with the morning." Lord, in the midst of my sorrow and depression, I seek the promise of joy that comes with Your new day.

I acknowledge my pain and sadness, yet I choose to cling to Your unfailing love and mercy. As the dawn breaks, let it bring a renewal of hope in my heart. Remind me that this period of darkness is only temporary, and that Your light is powerful enough to overcome the deepest despair.

Strengthen me, O God, to endure the challenges of each day. Fill me with the peace that surpasses all understanding, and guide my steps towards recovery. May Your grace be sufficient for me, and may Your power be made perfect in my weakness.

In Jesus' name, I pray

Amen.

Prayer 8: The Peace of God (Philippians 4:7)

Lord God,

In my struggle with depression, I draw near to Your promise in Philippians 4:7, "And the peace of God, which surpasses all understanding, will guard your hearts and your minds in Christ Jesus." In these challenging times, I long for the peace that only You can provide.

Grant me the serenity to accept the things I cannot change, and the courage to change the things I can. Help me to find solace in Your presence, knowing that You are with me in every step of this journey. May Your peace fill my heart, calming the turmoil within and providing a refuge from the storm of emotions.

Encourage me, O Lord, to reach out for support when needed, to share my burdens with those who care, and to remember that I am not alone in this fight. Teach me to rest in Your love, to find joy in Your creation, and to hold onto hope in the midst of despair.

In Jesus' name, I pray

Amen.

Prayer 9: Cast My Burden (Psalm 55:22)

Dear Heavenly Father, as I grapple with the weight of depression, I am comforted by the words of Psalm 55:22, "Cast your burden on the Lord, and He will sustain you; He will never permit the righteous to be moved." Today, I cast all my worries, fears, and sorrows upon You, trusting in Your strength to sustain me.

Help me, O God, to recognize the beauty and value in each day, even when clouded by sadness. Teach me to lean on You, to find rest in Your loving arms, and to trust in Your plan for my life. Let me be reminded that my journey, though difficult, is not without purpose, and that You are using my trials to shape me into the person You desire me to be.

May Your love envelop me, Your wisdom guide me, and Your comfort soothe my aching heart. Bring healing to my mind, body, and soul, and lead me out of this valley of despair into the light of Your hope and joy.

In Jesus' name, I pray

Amen.

Prayer 10: Out of the Depths (Psalm 130:1)

Dear Heavenly Father, as I stand in the depths of my despair, I am drawn to the words of Psalm 130:1, "Out of the depths I cry to you, O Lord." In this time of darkness, I turn to You, seeking Your light and guidance.

Lord, my heart is heavy, and my spirit feels weak. I am surrounded by shadows, and it seems hard to find the way forward. Yet, I trust in Your unfailing love and mercy. I believe that with You, even the darkest night will lead to dawn.

Strengthen me with Your grace, and help me to hold onto hope. Teach me to find solace in Your promises, and comfort in Your presence. May I remember that my journey through depression is not a path I walk alone, but one where You are always by my side, guiding and supporting me.

In Jesus' name, I pray

Amen.

Prayer 11: Healing for the Brokenhearted (Psalm 147:3)

Merciful God, I find solace in Your word, Psalm 147:3, "He heals the brokenhearted and binds up their wounds." As I struggle with the weight of depression, I seek Your healing touch upon my life.

My heart is shattered, and my soul feels bruised. The road to recovery seems long and uncertain. Yet, I believe in Your power to heal and restore. I place my broken pieces into Your hands, trusting that You can make me whole again.

Guide me through this valley of sorrow. Provide me with the strength to face each day, and the courage to take each step. Surround me with Your love and light, and lead me towards a brighter future filled with hope and peace.

In Jesus' name, I pray, Amen.

Prayer 12: A Future and a Hope (Jeremiah 29:11)

Almighty God, as I navigate the challenges of depression, I hold onto Your promise in Jeremiah 29:11,

"For I know the plans I have for you, declares the Lord, plans for welfare and not for evil, to give you a future and a hope." In this difficult season, I cling to the hope that You have plans for my good.

Despite the darkness that surrounds me, help me to see glimpses of the future You have prepared for me. Renew my mind and spirit, and fill me with a sense of purpose and direction. May I trust in Your timing and Your perfect plan for my life.

Empower me to rise above my circumstances, to find strength in Your love, and to walk in the confidence that comes from knowing You are in control. May my journey through depression lead to a deeper faith and a stronger relationship with You.

In Jesus' name, I pray,

Amen.

Personal notes:

_____

_____

_____

_____

_____

_____

_____

_____

_____

_____

_____

_____

_____

_____

_____

_____

_____

Prayers for Anger

The devil and his agents often use anger as a tool to disrupt your spiritual, emotional, and relational well-being. **Ephesians 4:26-27** says, *"In your anger do not sin: Do not let the sun go down while you are still angry, and do not give the devil a foothold."* This verse highlights how unresolved anger can be exploited by the devil to create division and strife. Anger can cloud your judgment, lead to hurtful actions, and damage your relationships with others and with God.

Overcoming Anger with Faith- To combat the devil's use of anger, it is essential to rely on God's guidance and practice forgiveness and patience. **James 1:19-20** advises, *"My dear brothers and sisters, take note of this: Everyone should be quick to listen, slow to speak and slow to become angry, because human anger does not produce the righteousness that God desires."* This verse encourages you to manage your anger in a way that aligns with God's will.

Prayer 1: A Heart at Peace" (Proverbs 14:29)

Heavenly Father,

Guided by Proverbs 14:29, "Whoever is slow to anger has great understanding," I seek Your help in controlling my anger. Grant me the patience and wisdom to respond with calmness and thoughtfulness, even in challenging situations.

May Your peace fill my heart, steering me away from hasty reactions and leading me toward understanding and compassion. Help me to listen more, speak less, and reflect Your love in my actions.

In Jesus' name, I pray,

Amen.

Prayer 2: Be Quick to Listen (James 1:19)

Lord, I embrace the teaching of James 1:19, "Everyone should be quick to listen, slow to speak and slow to become angry." Help me to truly listen and understand others, restraining my tongue and temper.

Instill in me the strength to be patient and the humility to seek reconciliation when anger tries to take hold. May I be an example of Your grace and love in all my interactions.

In Jesus' name, I pray

Amen.

Prayer 3: Fruits of the Spirit" (Galatians 5:22-23)

Dear God, as I strive to manage my anger, I recall Galatians 5:22-23, which speaks of the fruits of the Spirit. Fill me with love, joy, peace, patience, kindness, goodness, faithfulness, gentleness, and self-control.

Help me to embody these virtues in my daily life, especially when faced with situations that test my patience and tempt me towards anger. Guide me to act in ways that honor You and bring peace to those around me.

In Jesus' name, I pray

Amen.

Prayer 4: Path to Patience (Proverbs 15:18)

Heavenly Father, I seek guidance in the wisdom of Proverbs 15:18, "A hot-tempered person stirs up conflict, but the one who is patient calms a quarrel." Help me to cultivate patience and understanding in moments of frustration and anger.

Guide my words and actions to reflect Your love and peace. May I be an instrument of calm in times of strife, bringing resolution and understanding, rather than discord.

In Jesus' name, I pray

Amen.

Prayer 5: Slow to Anger (James 1:19)

Lord, as James 1:19 teaches, "Everyone should be quick to listen, slow to speak and slow to become angry," I pray for the strength to control my temper. Help me to listen with empathy, speak with kindness, and act with wisdom.

In moments of potential conflict, remind me of Your love and patience, so that I may extend the same to others. May my actions and words always be in alignment with Your teachings of compassion and understanding.

In Jesus' name, I pray, Amen.

Prayer 6: Spirit of Self-Control" (Galatians 5:22-23)

Dear God,

Inspired by Galatians 5:22-23, I ask for Your help in cultivating the fruit of the Spirit in my life, especially self-control. In moments of anger, help me to pause, reflect, and choose actions that bring peace and healing.

Grant me the wisdom to understand the root of my anger and the courage to address it constructively. May my words and actions be guided by Your love and grace, creating harmony and understanding.

In Jesus' name, I pray, Amen.

Prayer 7: Bridle of Peace" (James 1:19-20)

Heavenly Father, inspired by James 1:19-20, "Everyone should be quick to listen, slow to speak and slow to become angry, because human anger does not produce the righteousness that God desires," I come before You acknowledging my struggle with anger. It's a flame that can too easily be fanned into destructive wildfire, harming myself and those around me. Grant me the grace to be quick to listen and slow to anger, that I may seek understanding and peace rather than conflict.

I pray for Your wisdom to discern the root of my anger, to address it with Your guidance, and not to let it lead me into sin. Help me to express my feelings in ways that are constructive and healing, fostering dialogue and reconciliation. Let Your Spirit guide my words and actions, turning potential moments of anger into opportunities for growth and deeper connection with others.

Teach me to let go of anger and to embrace forgiveness, as You have forgiven us. May the peace of Christ rule in my heart, acting as a bridle to my emotions and a guide to my actions. Let me be an instrument of Your peace in a world that needs understanding and compassion, reflecting Your love and patience in all I do.

In Jesus' name, I pray,

Amen.

Prayer 8: The Path of Patience"
(Colossians 3:12-13)

Lord, Colossians 3:12-13 reminds us, "Therefore, as God's chosen people, holy and dearly loved, clothe yourselves with compassion, kindness, humility, gentleness and patience. Bear with each other and forgive one another if any of you has a grievance against someone." In the face of anger and frustration, I ask for the strength to clothe myself with patience and humility. Let me remember that everyone is fighting their own battles, and kindness can often be the balm that soothes the weary soul.

Instill in me a heart of compassion that looks beyond my immediate reactions to see the needs and struggles of others. Help me to practice patience, not only as a virtue but as a manifestation of Your love within me. Guide me in understanding and patience, allowing me to forgive as I have been forgiven, and to extend grace where it is needed most.

As I walk through daily life, let me be mindful of the power of my words and actions. May I choose to respond to others with gentleness and restraint, even in moments of provocation. In cultivating patience, let me also cultivate peace–within myself, in my relationships, and in my interactions with the world around me.

In Jesus' name, I pray

Amen.

Prayer 9: Harbor of Calm" (Proverbs 15:1)

Merciful Savior, Proverbs 15:1 teaches, "A gentle answer turns away wrath, but a harsh word stirs up anger." I seek Your guidance to be a harbor of calm in the stormy seas of anger. When emotions run high and the tempest of temper threatens to take control, remind me of the power of a gentle response. May my words be lighthouses of peace, guiding those lost in anger back to the shores of reason and understanding.

Empower me to face anger not with opposition, but with the calm assurance that comes from trusting in You. Let me understand the fears and hurts that often lie beneath anger, both in myself and in others. In offering a gentle answer, let me be a conduit of Your grace, diffusing tension and paving the way for healing and reconciliation.

In moments of anger, whether directed at me or emanating from within, let me turn to You for strength and guidance. Teach me to pause, to pray, and to proceed with love. May my life be a testament to the transforming power of Your love, showing that even in the midst of conflict, there can be a harbor of calm, a place of forgiveness, and a new beginning.

In Jesus' name, I pray

Amen.

Personal notes:

_____

_____

_____

_____

_____

_____

_____

_____

_____

_____

_____

_____

_____

_____

_____

_____

Prayers for Stress

The devil and his agents often use stress as a means to undermine your spiritual and emotional well-being. In **Matthew 11:28**, Jesus invites you, *"Come to me, all you who are weary and burdened, and I will give you rest."* This verse emphasizes the importance of finding rest and peace in Jesus, rather than succumbing to the pressures and anxieties of life. The devil seeks to exploit stress by overwhelming you with worries and fears, causing you to feel burdened and distracted from your faith. This can lead to a sense of hopelessness and a weakened connection with God, as stress consumes your thoughts and diverts your focus from His promises.

To counter the devil's use of stress, it is essential to rely on God's strength and guidance. **Philippians 4:6-7** advises, *"Do not be anxious about anything, but in every situation, by prayer and petition, with thanksgiving, present your requests to God. And the peace of God, which transcends all understanding, will guard your hearts and your minds in Christ Jesus."* This verse encourages you to turn to God in times of stress, seeking His peace through prayer and gratitude. By focusing on God's faithfulness and maintaining a thankful heart, you can overcome the negative effects of stress.

Prayer 1: In Quiet Waters (Psalm 23:2)

Heavenly Father, as the shepherd leads his flock to quiet waters, as expressed in Psalm 23:2, guide me to the stillness of Your presence amidst the chaos of my stress. In these turbulent times, let me find solace in Your nurturing care, where my soul is restored and my worries are calmed. As the waters are still, so too, may my heart find tranquility in Your loving embrace.

In the quietude of Your sanctuary, renew my spirit. Grant me the serenity to face my challenges with grace, and the wisdom to discern the path You have set before me. With each step, fortify my trust in Your guidance, knowing that You are with me, easing my burdens and illuminating my journey with hope and peace.

In Jesus' name, I pray, Amen.

Prayer 2: Cast All Anxieties" (1 Peter 5:7)

Lord, in alignment with the message of 1 Peter 5:7, "Cast all your anxiety on him because he cares for you," I lay down my stresses and fears at Your feet. In moments of overwhelming pressure, remind me that You are my steadfast supporter, ready to bear the weight of my concerns. May my heart find courage and comfort in

Your unending care, releasing the grip of stress that so often seeks to overwhelm me.

Transform my anxious thoughts into prayers of trust and reliance on You. As I navigate through the complexities of life, help me to maintain a perspective anchored in faith, not fear. Strengthen me with Your love, enabling me to face each day with renewed confidence and calm, secure in the knowledge that I am under Your watchful care and loving protection.

In Jesus' name, I pray, Amen.

Prayer 3: Shelter of Peace" (Philippians 4:6-7)

Merciful God, inspired by Philippians 4:6-7, which urges us to be anxious for nothing but in everything by prayer and supplication, with thanksgiving, to let our requests be known to God, I seek Your shelter of peace. In the midst of life's storms, where stress and worry threaten to overwhelm, be my refuge where calmness reigns and anxiety dissipates. Let Your peace, which surpasses all understanding, guard my heart and mind through Christ Jesus.

In Your presence, may the tumult of my thoughts be stilled and the chaos of my circumstances be subdued.

Provide me with the strength to persevere, the faith to trust, and the resilience to thrive. May each breath I take be filled with Your tranquility, and every step I take be aligned with Your divine wisdom, leading me to a place of balance and harmony.

In Jesus' name, I pray

Amen.

Prayer 4: Rest for the Weary (Matthew 11:28)

Heavenly Father, in the spirit of Matthew 11:28, "Come to me, all who are weary and burdened, and I will give you rest," I seek Your solace in my stress. In these moments of overwhelm, remind me that You offer a sanctuary for the weary. Help me to lay down my burdens at Your feet and find rest in Your loving embrace.

Rejuvenate my spirit, Lord. As I rest in You, renew my strength and provide me with the courage to face the challenges before me. Let Your peace envelop me, shielding me from the anxieties of the world.

In Jesus' name, I pray, **Amen.**

Prayer 5: Strength in Stillness (Psalm 46:10)

Lord God, echoing Psalm 46:10, "Be still, and know that I am God," I ask for the serenity amidst life's storms. In times of stress and uncertainty, help me to find stillness in Your presence. Teach me to quiet my mind and trust in Your sovereign control over my life.

In the stillness, may I recognize Your guiding hand. Strengthen my faith and my resolve, enabling me to approach my responsibilities and challenges with a calm and focused mind, rooted in the assurance of Your unfailing love.

In Jesus' name, I pray, Amen.

Prayer 6: Guidance Through Trials (James 1:2-4)

Dear God, inspired by James 1:2-4, "Consider it pure joy, my brothers and sisters, whenever you face trials of many kinds," I seek Your guidance through the stress and trials of my life. Help me to view these challenges as opportunities to grow stronger in my faith and closer to You.

Grant me the wisdom to navigate these trials with grace and perseverance. Let Your joy be my strength, and Your promise of growth and endurance be the anchor for my soul. May I emerge from these challenges with a deeper understanding of Your love and purpose for me.

In Jesus' name, I pray, Amen.

Prayer 7: Footsteps in the Sand (Psalm 77:19)

Heavenly Father, as I traverse the challenging terrains of life, I am reminded of Psalm 77:19, "Your path led through the sea, your way through the mighty waters, though your footprints were not seen." In these moments of stress and uncertainty, help me to trust in Your unseen guidance. Though I may not always discern Your footprints alongside mine, I am comforted knowing You are leading the way, parting the tumultuous seas that stand before me.

Grant me the faith, Lord, to follow where You lead, even when the path seems shrouded in mist. Strengthen my resolve, and infuse my spirit with peace, knowing that every step I take is ordained by Your divine wisdom. May Your unwavering presence be the compass that guides me through the storms, and Your word the light that illuminates my path, bringing clarity and direction amidst the chaos of life.

In Jesus' name, I pray, Amen.

Prayer 8: Unburdened Hearts (Matthew 11:28-30)

Dear Lord Jesus, I draw near to You, echoing the comfort of Matthew 11:28-30, "Come to me, all who are weary and burdened, and I will give you rest." In this world full of stress and relentless demands, I seek refuge in Your loving embrace. Lift the heavy yoke from my shoulders, replace it with Your light and easy one, and let me find true rest in Your presence. As I lay my burdens at Your feet, replace my anxiety with Your peace, my turmoil with Your calm.

Teach me, Lord, to walk in Your ways and to find joy in the simplicity of Your love. Help me to understand that in You, I find the strength to face each day, not burdened by the weight of the world, but uplifted by Your grace and love. May Your peace, which surpasses all understanding, guard my heart and mind, keeping me serene and focused on the things of eternal significance.

In Jesus' name, I pray, Amen.

Prayer 9: The Peace of God (Philippians 4:6-7)

Merciful God, in accordance with Philippians 4:6-7, "Do not be anxious about anything, but in every situation, by prayer and petition, with thanksgiving, present your requests to God," I come before You. Amidst the whirlwind of my daily tasks and responsibilities, the stress and pressures of life, I seek the peace of God which transcends all understanding. May this divine peace guard my heart and mind in Christ Jesus, anchoring me in the midst of life's storms.

Help me, O Lord, to lay down my worries at the foot of the cross, entrusting them into Your capable hands. Teach me to live each day with gratitude, recognizing the multitude of blessings that surround me, even in the midst of trials. Strengthen my faith, so that in every situation, whether in abundance or in need, I can experience the profound peace that comes from knowing You are in control and that Your love for me is unchanging.

In Jesus' name, I pray

Amen.

Prayer 10: In the Shelter of the Most High (Psalm 91:1)

Heavenly Father, as I dwell in the shelter of the Most High, as expressed in Psalm 91:1, I seek refuge from the stress that overwhelms me. In the shadow of Your wings, let me find a haven of peace and security. The pressures of life, the endless demands, and the relentless pace often leave me feeling weary and burdened. In these moments, I look to You for strength and solace, trusting in Your unfailing love and protection.

As I navigate through the complexities of my daily life, help me to remember that You are my fortress and my sanctuary. In the midst of chaos, remind me to breathe and to find stillness in Your presence. Teach me to lay down my worries at Your feet and to find rest for my soul. May I be anchored in Your peace, drawing comfort from the knowledge that You are always with me, guiding my steps and providing for my needs.

Lord, renew my spirit with Your calming presence. Fill me with the assurance that, under Your watchful eye, I am safe and cared for. Help me to cast my anxieties upon You, for You bear my burdens with a loving heart. As I rest in Your shelter, may my heart be lifted in gratitude and my mind eased from the stresses of life.

In Jesus' name, I pray, Amen.

Prayer 11: Rivers of Living Water (John 7:38)

Dear Lord, in the words of John 7:38, "Whoever believes in me, as Scripture has said, rivers of living water will flow from within them," I seek Your refreshing presence in my life. The stresses and strains I face each day often feel like a desert, parched and lifeless. I long for the rivers of Your peace and joy to flow through me, revitalizing my spirit and quenching the thirst of my soul.

In moments of stress and pressure, remind me to turn to You, the source of all comfort and strength. Help me to draw deeply from Your well of living water, finding in You the sustenance and nourishment my soul needs. Teach me to rely not on my own understanding but to trust in Your wise and perfect plan for my life. Guide me in paths of righteousness, leading me beside still waters and restoring my soul.

Grant me the wisdom to discern the important from the urgent, and the courage to say no to the demands that drain my spirit. May Your living water flow through me, bringing life and hope to every area of my existence. Let Your peace reign in my heart, dispelling stress and anxiety, and filling me with a sense of purpose and contentment.

In Jesus' name, I pray, Amen.

Prayer 12: Unwavering Faith Amidst the Storm" (Matthew 8:26)

Merciful Savior, in the midst of life's storms, as You calmed the winds and the waves in Matthew 8:26, I seek Your calming presence in my life. The storms of stress and anxiety often rage around me, threatening to overwhelm my peace and stability. In these turbulent times, I look to You, my anchor and my shield, to bring stillness to my restless heart and mind.

Help me, Lord, to keep my eyes fixed on You, trusting in Your power and love to guide me through. Teach me to find strength in Your promises, comfort in Your presence, and hope in Your unfailing grace. Amidst the pressures of work, family, and daily responsibilities, remind me that You are the master of the sea and the commander of the winds. With You, I can weather any storm.

Strengthen my faith, O God, that I may not falter or be swayed by the tempests of life. Infuse my being with Your peace, the peace that surpasses all understanding. As I trust in You, transform my anxiety into tranquility, my fear into courage, and my stress into serenity. May Your love be the beacon that guides me through the darkest hours and Your wisdom the light that illuminates my path.

In Jesus' name, I pray

Amen.

Personal notes:

_____

_____

_____

_____

_____

_____

_____

_____

_____

_____

_____

_____

_____

_____

_____

_____

_____

_____

Prayers for Spiritual Warfare

The devil uses spiritual warfare to attack and weaken you by targeting your faith, mind, and emotions. In **Ephesians 6:12**, the Bible states, "*For our struggle is not against flesh and blood, but against the rulers, against the authorities, against the powers of this dark world and against the spiritual forces of evil in the heavenly realms.*" This verse highlights the reality of spiritual warfare and the unseen battles you face daily. The devil employs various tactics, such as deception, temptation, and accusations, to create doubt, fear, and confusion in your life. By undermining your trust in God and distorting your perception of truth, the devil aims to disrupt your relationship with God and hinder your spiritual growth.

Overcoming Spiritual Warfare: to combat the devil's use of spiritual warfare, it is crucial to put on the full armor of God as described in **Ephesians 6:13-17**. This passage encourages you to "*take up the shield of faith, with which you can extinguish all the flaming arrows of the evil one.*" Strengthening your faith and grounding yourself in God's word, you can resist the devil's attacks and stand firm in your beliefs. Engaging in regular prayer, studying the scriptures, and maintaining fellowship with other believers are vital strategies in overcoming spiritual warfare.

Prayer 1: Armor of God (Ephesians 6:11)

Heavenly Father, as Ephesians 6:11 instructs, "Put on the full armor of God, so that you can take your stand against the devil's schemes." I come before You seeking strength and protection in this spiritual battle. Clothe me with Your armor - the belt of truth, the breastplate of righteousness, the gospel of peace, the shield of faith, the helmet of salvation, and the sword of the Spirit. Let these armaments shield me from the enemy's attacks and empower me to stand firm in Your truth.

Equip me, Lord, to discern the subtle deceptions and to resist the temptations that come my way. In moments of weakness, remind me that Your power is made perfect. Strengthen my resolve and deepen my faith, that I may emerge victorious in the spiritual battles I face daily.

In Jesus' name, I pray,

Amen.

Prayer 2: Victory in Christ (1 Corinthians 15:57)

Dear Lord,

Inspired by 1 Corinthians 15:57, "But thanks be to God! He gives us the victory through our Lord Jesus Christ," I approach this spiritual warfare with confidence in Your victory. In the midst of trials and temptations, help me to remember that the battle is already won through Christ. May I rely on His strength and wisdom to navigate the challenges and spiritual attacks that come my way.

Keep me grounded in Your Word and steadfast in prayer, Lord. May my heart always be aligned with Your will, my actions a reflection of Your love, and my life a testament to Your grace. In every spiritual struggle, remind me that I am more than a conqueror through Him who loves me.

In Jesus' name, I pray, Amen.

Prayer 3: Light Overcomes Darkness (John 1:5)

Merciful God, as John 1:5 declares, "The light shines in the darkness, and the darkness has not overcome it," I pray for Your light to guide and protect me in spiritual warfare. In the face of darkness and evil, let Your truth and love be the beacon that guides my path. Shield me from the snares of the enemy and fortify my spirit with Your divine light.

In times of doubt and fear, illuminate my path with the light of Your Word. Let Your presence be a constant source of comfort and strength. Teach me to trust in Your sovereign power, knowing that no force of darkness can withstand the brilliance of Your light. May I walk confidently in the knowledge that in You, light always overcomes darkness.

In Jesus' name, I pray,

Amen.

Prayer 4: Stand Firm in Faith (Ephesians 6:13)

Heavenly Father, guided by Ephesians 6:13, "Therefore put on the full armor of God, so that when the day of evil comes, you may be able to stand your ground," I seek Your strength in this spiritual battle. Equip me with Your armor, that I may stand firm against the schemes of the enemy. In the face of temptation and spiritual attack, let Your truth be my shield and Your word my sword.

Strengthen my faith, Lord, that I may resist the devil and his deceptions. Help me to walk in Your ways, keeping my eyes fixed on Jesus, the author, and perfecter of my faith. May I stand unwavering in Your truth, empowered by Your Spirit to overcome the challenges of this spiritual warfare.

In Jesus' name, I pray,

Amen.

Prayer 5: The Victory is Ours (1 John 5:4-5)

Lord God, as 1 John 5:4-5 declares, "For everyone born of God overcomes the world," I trust in Your promise of victory. In this spiritual struggle, remind me that I am born of God and that the victory is already won through Jesus Christ. Let this assurance give me strength and courage to face and overcome the trials and temptations that arise.

I pray for wisdom and discernment in this battle, knowing that You are with me every step of the way. Help me to cling to Your word and to rely on Your strength, not my own. May I be a beacon of Your light in the darkness, confidently proclaiming Your victory over sin and death.

In Jesus' name, I pray

Amen.

Prayer 6: Light in Darkness (John 1:5)

Merciful Savior, inspired by John 1:5, "The light shines in the darkness, and the darkness has not overcome it," I pray for Your light to guide me in the midst of spiritual warfare. In times of doubt and struggle, shine Your light upon me, dispelling the darkness of fear and confusion. Let Your truth illuminate my path and guide my steps.

Protect me from the snares of the enemy, and surround me with Your heavenly hosts. May Your presence be a constant source of comfort and strength. In the battle against spiritual darkness, help me to remember that Your light will always prevail, and in You, there is no darkness at all.

In Jesus' name, I pray, Amen.

Prayer 7: Shield of Faith (Ephesians 6:16)

Heavenly Father, as Ephesians 6:16 instructs, "In all circumstances take up the shield of faith, with which you can extinguish all the flaming darts of the evil one." I come before You in this time of spiritual warfare, seeking Your protection and strength. Equip me with the shield of faith, that I may stand strong against the onslaught of the enemy and extinguish his fiery arrows.

Lord, increase my faith in these challenging times. Help me to trust in Your promises and Your power, standing firm in the belief that no weapon formed against me shall prosper. Let my faith be the barrier that shields me from doubt, fear, and despair.

In the heat of battle, remind me that my strength comes from You. May I be steadfast in my faith, unwavering in the face of adversity, and confident in Your victory over all the forces of darkness.

In Jesus' name, I pray, Amen.

Prayer 8: The Sword of the Spirit (Ephesians 6:17)

Dear Lord, guided by Ephesians 6:17, "Take the helmet of salvation and the sword of the Spirit, which is the word of God," I ask for Your empowerment in this spiritual struggle. Let Your Word be my sword, cutting through deception and revealing the truth. May I wield this sword skillfully, fortified by Your wisdom and understanding.

In moments of doubt and confusion, let Your Word be the light that guides my path. Help me to immerse myself in Scripture, drawing strength and courage from its truths. May Your promises and teachings be the foundation upon which I stand, unshaken by the enemy's lies.

Teach me, O God, to use Your Word not only as a weapon of defense but also as a tool of love and grace. Let me speak Your truth in love, being an instrument of Your peace and righteousness in the midst of spiritual battles.

In Jesus' name, I pray

Amen.

Prayer 9: Overcomers Through Christ (Romans 8:37)

Merciful Savior, in the spirit of Romans 8:37, "In all these things we are more than conquerors through him who loved us," I approach this spiritual warfare with confidence in Your love and power. Remind me that in You, I have the strength to overcome every spiritual obstacle and trial. In the face of adversity, let Your love be my constant source of courage and hope.

Equip me, Lord, to face the battles of this day with the assurance of Your presence and guidance. Help me to recognize the enemy's tactics and to stand firm in my faith, clothed in the armor of God. May my heart be steadfast, trusting in Your ultimate victory over sin and death.

In every challenge, let me draw upon the power of Your Spirit. Strengthen me to resist temptation, to stand for truth, and to walk in the light of Your grace and mercy. May my life reflect Your love and triumph over the powers of darkness.

In Jesus' name, I pray, Amen.

Prayer 10: Conquer Through Christ (Romans 8:37)

Heavenly Father, as Romans 8:37 proclaims, "We are more than conquerors through Him who loved us." In the midst of spiritual warfare, I lean on this profound truth. Your love empowers me to face and overcome the forces that stand against me. Remind me, Lord, that in You, I possess the strength to conquer fear, doubt, and every spiritual adversary.

Equip me with Your spiritual armor. Let the helmet of salvation protect my thoughts, the breastplate of righteousness guard my heart, and the belt of truth uphold my spirit. May the shield of faith extinguish the fiery darts of the enemy, and the sword of the Spirit, which is Your Word, be my defense and offense against the lies and deceptions of the adversary.

I stand firm, rooted in Your promise of victory. Strengthen my resolve, deepen my faith, and increase my reliance on Your power. In every battle, let me find refuge in Your presence, assurance in Your promises, and boldness in Your name. I claim victory over the enemy, not by my might, but through the power of Your love and the grace of Jesus Christ.

In Jesus' name, I pray, Amen.

Prayer 11: Victory in the Light (John 1:5)

Lord Jesus, John 1:5 declares, "The light shines in the darkness, and the darkness has not overcome it." In this spiritual battle, I embrace Your light as my guide and shield. Dispel the darkness around me, and let Your truth illuminate my path. In the shadow of adversity, remind me that Your light is ever-present, revealing the way and bringing hope to my journey.

Strengthen my resolve to walk in Your light, resisting the temptations and lies of the enemy. Let Your light shine through me, becoming a beacon of hope and truth to those engulfed in darkness. In times of confusion and deceit, may I discern Your will and remain steadfast in Your truth.

Your light, O Lord, is my assurance in this spiritual warfare. No darkness can withstand Your radiant presence. Guard my heart, guide my steps, and use me as an instrument of Your peace and light. With confidence and trust, I step forward, knowing that victory is found in Your eternal light.

In Jesus' name, I pray,

Amen.

Prayer 12: God's Armor (Ephesians 6:11)

Heavenly Father, in the spirit of Ephesians 6:11, "Put on the full armor of God, so that you can take your stand against the devil's schemes," I seek Your protection and strength. As I face the trials and temptations of this world, clothe me in Your armor. Let the belt of truth, the breastplate of righteousness, the gospel of peace, the shield of faith, the helmet of salvation, and the sword of the Spirit be my defense and my strength.

In this spiritual warfare, help me to stand firm in faith and truth. Equip me with discernment to recognize the enemy's tactics and wisdom to counteract them. May I remain grounded in Your Word, drawing strength from its promises and guidance for each battle I face.

I place my trust in You, Lord. With Your armor, I am prepared to face any challenge, confident in Your power and guidance. Strengthen me to stand firm, to fight the good fight, and to emerge victorious, proclaiming Your glory and Your sovereignty over all spiritual forces.

In Jesus' name, I pray, Amen.

Prayer 13: The Full Armor of God (Ephesians 6:11)

Heavenly Father, as Ephesians 6:11 exhorts, "Put on the full armor of God, so that you can take your stand against the devil's schemes," I come to You in need of Your strength and protection. In the midst of this spiritual battle, clothe me with Your armor. Let the belt of truth, the breastplate of righteousness, and the shoes of peace prepare me to stand firm in faith.

Empower me, Lord, with the shield of faith to quench the fiery darts of the enemy, the helmet of salvation to guard my thoughts, and the sword of the Spirit, which is Your Word, to combat lies and temptations. With Your armor, I am equipped to face every challenge, secure in the victory that is mine through Christ Jesus.

In Jesus' name, I pray

Amen.

Prayer 14: Overcoming in Christ (Romans 8:37)

Lord God, inspired by Romans 8:37, "In all these things we are more than conquerors through him who loved us," I affirm my victory in spiritual warfare through Christ. In the face of trials and temptations, remind me that I am not fighting in my own strength, but in the power of Your love and grace.

Strengthen my faith and resolve, so I may resist and overcome the wiles of the enemy. Let Your love be my shield and Your truth my guide, as I navigate through the challenges of this spiritual journey. In Christ, I stand confident and assured, claiming victory over every spiritual obstacle.

In Jesus' name, I pray

Amen.

Prayer 15: Light in the Darkness (John 1:5)

Merciful Savior, as John 1:5 declares, "The light shines in the darkness, and the darkness has not overcome it," I seek Your illumination in my spiritual battles. In moments of doubt and struggle, shine Your light upon my path, dispelling fear and confusion with the truth of Your Word.

Surround me with Your presence, O Lord, as I confront the forces of darkness. Let Your wisdom guide my decisions, and Your peace calm my spirit. In the assurance of Your light, I step forward boldly, knowing that no darkness can withstand the power of Your radiant glory.

In Jesus' name, I pray

Amen.

Personal notes:

_____

_____

_____

_____

_____

_____

_____

_____

_____

_____

_____

_____

_____

_____

_____

_____

Prayers for Deliverance

Your deliverance has a profound impact on your life, transforming you spiritually, emotionally, and even physically. In **2 Corinthians 5:17**, the Bible states, **"*Therefore, if anyone is in Christ, the new creation has come: The old has gone, the new is here!*"** This verse highlights the transformative power of deliverance through Christ, emphasizing that you are made new. Deliverance frees you from the chains of sin, fear, and oppression, allowing you to experience the fullness of God's love and grace. As a result, you gain a renewed sense of purpose, peace, and joy that permeates every aspect of your life.

Living in the freedom of your deliverance means embracing the new life that Christ has given you and walking in the victory He has won. Galatians 5:1 encourages you, "It is for freedom that Christ has set us free. Stand firm, then, and do not let yourselves be burdened again by a yoke of slavery." This verse urges you to remain steadfast in your freedom and not fall back into old patterns of bondage.

Prayer 1: Set Free in Christ (John 8:36)

Heavenly Father, as John 8:36 declares, "So if the Son sets you free, you will be free indeed." I seek Your deliverance from the chains that bind me. In my struggles and the areas of my life where I feel captive, I pray for the freedom that comes only through Jesus Christ. Break the bonds of fear, doubt, and sin that entangle me.

Grant me the courage and strength to walk in the liberty provided by Your Son. Fill my heart with the assurance that in Christ, I am released from the past and empowered to embrace the future You have planned for me. Let Your light guide me to paths of righteousness and peace.

In Jesus' name, I pray

Amen.

Prayer 2: God, Our Deliverer (Psalm 18:2)

Lord God, I call upon You as my rock and deliverer, as expressed in Psalm 18:2, "The Lord is my rock, my fortress, and my deliverer." In times of trouble and distress, I look to You for rescue. Deliver me from the trials that overwhelm my spirit and the temptations that threaten my faith.

Shield me with Your strength and guide me to safety. Help me to trust in Your protection and to find solace in Your unfailing love. May I emerge from these trials stronger in faith, drawing ever closer to You, my rock and salvation.

In Jesus' name, I pray, Amen.

Prayer 3: Path of Redemption (Psalm 25:15)

Merciful Savior, according to Psalm 25:15, "My eyes are ever toward the Lord, for he will pluck my feet out of the net." I turn to You in my need for deliverance. From the snares and pitfalls that life sets before me, I seek Your guiding hand. Free me from the entanglements that hinder my walk with You.

Direct my steps, O Lord, and lead me in Your ways of righteousness. May Your grace and mercy be my constant companions, shielding me from harm and guiding me to a place of safety and restoration. In Your love, I find hope and the promise of a new beginning.

In Jesus' name, I pray, Amen.

Prayer 4: Deliver Us from Evil (Matthew 6:13)

Heavenly Father, as we are taught in the Lord's Prayer, "deliver us from evil" (Matthew 6:13), I seek Your powerful intervention. In the face of trials and tribulations, I call upon Your name for deliverance. Protect me from the snares of the enemy and the dangers that lurk in my path.

Guide me with Your wisdom and strength. Break the chains of any bondage that seeks to hold me back, and lead me into the freedom and peace found only in Your embrace. In every challenge, let me find solace and strength in Your unfailing love and power.

In Jesus' name, I pray, Amen.

Prayer 5: The Lord is My Helper (Hebrews 13:6)

Lord God, I hold onto the promise of Hebrews 13:6, "The Lord is my helper; I will not be afraid." In times of distress and uncertainty, be my refuge and strength. I ask for Your divine assistance to overcome the obstacles that stand before me.

Lift the weight of worry and fear from my heart. Replace it with Your courageous spirit, enabling me to face life's challenges with faith and confidence. May Your presence bring comfort and Your guidance light the way to a brighter and more hopeful path.

In Jesus' name, I pray, Amen.

Prayer 6: A New Creation (2 Corinthians 5:17)

Merciful Savior, inspired by 2 Corinthians 5:17, "Therefore, if anyone is in Christ, he is a new creation," I seek Your deliverance and transformation. In the struggles that bind me, I pray for the freedom and renewal that comes through faith in You.

Release me from past burdens and regrets, and renew my spirit. Let me embrace the new life You offer, filled with Your grace and truth. As a new creation in Christ, guide me to walk in Your ways, leaving behind what once was and moving forward in the hope and joy of what is now in You.

In Jesus' name, I pray,

Amen.

Prayer 7: Breaking the Chains (John 8:36)

Heavenly Father, inspired by John 8:36, "So if the Son sets you free, you will be free indeed," I come before You seeking deliverance. In the areas of my life where I am bound by fear, doubt, or sin, I pray for the freedom that only Your Son, Jesus Christ, can provide. Break the chains that hold me captive and release me into the liberty of Your grace.

Lord, guide me on the path to spiritual freedom. Shine Your light on the shadows within my heart and dispel the darkness with Your love. Help me to let go of the burdens that weigh me down, entrusting them to You, confident in Your power to heal and restore.

May Your peace, which surpasses all understanding, guard my heart and mind. In the freedom found in Christ, empower me to live a life that honors You, full of hope, joy, and gratitude. Lead me to walk in Your ways, embracing the fullness of life You offer.

In Jesus' name, I pray, Amen.

Prayer 8: Refuge and Strength (Psalm 46:1)

Lord God, as Psalm 46:1 says, "God is our refuge and strength, an ever-present help in trouble," I seek Your shelter in my time of need. In the midst of life's storms, be my refuge and strength. Deliver me from the difficulties I face, and provide a safe haven for my weary soul.

In Your presence, let me find solace and strength. Grant me the wisdom to navigate through my trials and the faith to trust in Your providence. Protect me from harm, and surround me with Your love and care.

Uphold me with Your righteous right hand, and guide me through the challenges that lie ahead. May I always remember that You are with me, my fortress in times of distress. Let Your faithfulness be my shield and comfort as I rely on Your unfailing love and power for deliverance.

In Jesus' name, I pray,

Amen.

Prayer 9: A Way in the Wilderness (Isaiah 43:19)

Merciful Savior, according to Isaiah 43:19, "I am making a way in the wilderness and streams in the wasteland," I call upon You for deliverance in my life. In the midst of what feels like a wilderness, make a way for me, Lord. Create streams of living water in the dry and weary lands of my soul, refreshing and renewing my spirit.

Guide me through the difficulties that surround me, and open my eyes to see the pathways You have set before me. Transform my struggles into opportunities for growth and deepen my trust in Your guidance and provision.

Strengthen my faith as I journey through this wilderness. Lead me to places of rest and restoration, and use my experiences to glorify Your name. In Your wisdom and love, provide a way where there seems to be no way, and guide me to a place of peace and deliverance.

In Jesus' name, I pray, Amen.

Prayer 10: Freedom in the Spirit (2 Corinthians 3:17)

Heavenly Father, as declared in 2 Corinthians 3:17, "Where the Spirit of the Lord is, there is freedom," I seek Your deliverance in the areas of my life where I feel bound. You know the struggles that weigh heavily on my heart, the chains of fear, doubt, and sin that hinder my walk with You. I ask for the freedom that Your Spirit brings, to break every chain and release me from the grip of anything that is not of You.

In Your mercy, Lord, shine Your light into the darkest corners of my life. Illuminate the paths of deliverance and guide my steps towards Your will. Grant me the courage to face my challenges, knowing that in Your presence, there is fullness of joy and peace. Help me to surrender my burdens to You, trusting in Your love and power to save.

May Your grace envelop me, and Your Spirit empower me to live a life of freedom and victory. As I walk in this newfound liberty, use my story to bring hope and encouragement to others who are struggling. Let my life be a testimony to Your redeeming power and love.

In Jesus' name, I pray, Amen.

Prayer 11: God of Breakthroughs (2 Samuel 5:20)

Lord Almighty, in the spirit of 2 Samuel 5:20, where You are referred to as "the Lord of breakthroughs," I approach Your throne seeking deliverance from the obstacles and barriers in my life. You are the God who breaks through the impossible, the One who makes a way where there seems to be no way. I bring before You the challenges that I cannot overcome on my own, asking for Your intervention and breakthrough.

Help me, O God, to have faith in Your power and timing. Teach me to wait patiently for Your deliverance, standing firm on Your promises. In moments of weakness, remind me of Your faithfulness and Your ability to bring victory in the midst of adversity. May I find strength in the knowledge that You are fighting for me, breaking down walls and clearing paths.

May my heart be filled with praise and thanksgiving for the victories You are about to bring. I trust in Your goodness and mercy, confident that You are working all things for my good. May my journey of deliverance showcase Your glory, and may my life reflect the breakthrough power of Your love and grace.

In Jesus' name, I pray, Amen.

Prayer 12: Title: "Restoration and Renewal" (Psalm 23:3)

Merciful Savior, guided by Psalm 23:3, "He restores my soul," I come to You in need of healing and renewal. In the midst of life's trials and pain, I seek Your comforting presence. Restore my weary soul, mend what is broken, and rejuvenate my spirit with Your healing touch.

In Your boundless compassion, renew my strength and hope. Lift the burdens that weigh heavily upon me and replace them with Your peace. Guide me along paths of righteousness, leading me back to a place of spiritual wholeness and health. In the valleys of despair, remind me that You are with me, Your rod and staff comforting me.

I place my trust in Your unfailing love and restorative power. May my life reflect the transformation You bring, shining as a beacon of Your faithfulness and grace. In every step of my journey, let me be a witness to the miracle of Your restorative love, bringing hope to others who are walking through their own valleys.

In Jesus' name, I pray

Amen.

Personal notes:

_____

_____

_____

_____

_____

_____

_____

_____

_____

_____

_____

_____

_____

_____

_____

_____

_____

_____

Prayers for Anxiety

The devil often uses anxiety to undermine your faith and well-being. In **1 Peter 5:7-8,** the Bible instructs, *"Cast all your anxiety on him because he cares for you. Be alert and of sober mind. Your enemy the devil prowls around like a roaring lion looking for someone to devour."* This passage emphasizes the importance of trusting God with your worries and being vigilant against the devil's schemes. The devil exploits anxiety by amplifying your fears and insecurities, causing you to feel overwhelmed and helpless. This constant state of worry can distract you from God's promises and disrupt your peace, making it difficult to focus on your spiritual growth and relationship with God.

Overcoming Anxiety with Faith: to combat the devil's use of anxiety, it is crucial to rely on God's strength and promises. **Philippians 4:6-7** encourages you, *"Do not be anxious about anything, but in every situation, by prayer and petition, with thanksgiving, present your requests to God. And the peace of God, which transcends all understanding, will guard your hearts and your minds in Christ Jesus."* This verse urges you to turn to God in times of anxiety, seeking His peace through prayer and gratitude. By focusing on God's faithfulness and maintaining a thankful heart, you can overcome the negative effects of anxiety.

Prayer 1: Peace That Surpasses Understanding (Philippians 4:7)

Heavenly Father, in line with Philippians 4:7, "And the peace of God, which surpasses all understanding, will guard your hearts and minds through Christ Jesus," I come to You with my anxious thoughts. In moments of worry and uncertainty, envelop me in Your peace that defies comprehension. Calm the storms within my mind and heart, replacing anxiety with Your profound tranquility.

Help me, Lord, to focus on Your promises and faithfulness. Let Your presence be a soothing balm to my restless spirit. May I find solace in Your Word and comfort in the knowledge that You are always by my side, guiding and protecting me.

In Jesus' name, I pray

Amen.

Prayer 2: Cast All Your Anxiety (1 Peter 5:7)

Dear Lord, as 1 Peter 5:7 encourages, "Cast all your anxiety on Him because He cares for you," I lay down my worries at Your feet. In the overwhelming tides of anxiety and fear, remind me that I can entrust every concern to You, knowing that You hold me in Your loving care.

Strengthen my faith to trust in Your timing and plan. In moments of stress, guide me to seek solace in prayer and in Your comforting presence. Let Your love and assurance be the anchor for my soul, keeping me grounded amidst life's uncertainties.

In Jesus' name, I pray, Amen.

Prayer 3: Do Not Be Anxious (Matthew 6:34)

Merciful Savior, echoing Matthew 6:34, "Therefore do not be anxious about tomorrow, for tomorrow will be anxious for itself," I seek Your help in releasing my worries. Help me to live in the present moment, trusting that You will take care of tomorrow. Relieve the burdens of anxiety from my shoulders, and instill in me a sense of peace and contentment.

Teach me, Lord, to place my concerns in Your capable hands. Guide my thoughts towards gratitude and positivity. May I be reminded of Your constant love and care, finding reassurance in Your promise to provide for all my needs according to Your riches and glory.

In Jesus' name, I pray, Amen.

Prayer 4: Casting All Your Cares (1 Peter 5:7)

Heavenly Father, in harmony with 1 Peter 5:7, "Cast all your anxiety on him because he cares for you," I lay before You my worries and fears. In these moments of anxiety, I choose to entrust every concern to Your loving care. Lift the weight of anxiety from my shoulders, replacing it with Your peace that surpasses all understanding.

Guide my heart and mind towards Your comforting presence. Remind me that in every situation, You are in control, and Your love is unceasing. May I find solace in Your promises, knowing that You are always with me, providing strength and comfort in times of need.

In Jesus' name, I pray, Amen.

Prayer 5: Do Not Be Anxious (Philippians 4:6)

Lord, as Philippians 4:6 encourages, "Do not be anxious about anything, but in every situation, by prayer and petition, with thanksgiving, present your requests to God," I bring to You my anxious thoughts. Help me to replace worry with prayer, doubt with faith, and fear with gratitude. May Your peace, which transcends all understanding, guard my heart and mind in Christ Jesus.

In moments of anxiety, let me find comfort in prayer and solace in Your loving arms. Strengthen my trust in Your providence and care. Let me rest in the assurance that You are always by my side, guiding me through each day with Your unfailing love and grace.

In Jesus' name, I pray, Amen.

Prayer 6: Be Still and Know (Psalm 46:10)

Merciful God, echoing Psalm 46:10, "Be still, and know that I am God," I seek stillness in Your presence amidst my anxiety. In the rush of life and the whirlwind of my thoughts, remind me to pause and recognize Your sovereignty. Calm my anxious mind and bring peace to my troubled heart.

Teach me to find rest in Your unchanging nature and comfort in Your steadfast love. May I learn to trust in Your plans and timings, knowing that You work all things for good. In the quietness of Your presence, renew my strength and fill me with Your peace.

In Jesus' name, I pray, Amen.

Prayer 7: Anchored in Hope (Hebrews 6:19)

Heavenly Father, as Hebrews 6:19 states, "We have this hope as an anchor for the soul, firm and secure," I come to You amidst the waves of anxiety and uncertainty. In moments of worry and fear, remind me that my hope is anchored in You. Your steadfast love and faithfulness are the rock on which I can stand, even when everything around me feels unsteady and tumultuous.

In the swirling currents of life, help me to focus on Your presence, which brings peace and stability. Calm my anxious thoughts, and replace my fears with the assurance of Your love and protection. May I find solace in the truth that You are always with me, guiding me through every storm.

Lord, strengthen my faith and trust in You. Teach me to rest in the security of Your promises, knowing that Your grace is sufficient for me. Let my heart be filled with peace as I lean on Your understanding, not my own, and may Your hope be the anchor that holds me steady in every circumstance.

In Jesus' name, I pray

Amen.

Prayer 8: Cast Your Cares (1 Peter 5:7)

Dear Lord, echoing the words of 1 Peter 5:7, "Cast all your anxiety on him because he cares for you," I lay before You all that troubles my heart. In the grip of anxiety, I choose to release my worries into Your caring hands. Knowing that You are ever-present and always caring, I seek relief and comfort in Your embrace.

Guide me to trust in Your sovereign care and provision. In moments of heightened anxiety, remind me that You are in control, and that my concerns are known to You. Replace my restless thoughts with Your peace, and my uncertainty with Your assurance. Let me feel Your presence and find strength in Your unending love.

Strengthen my resolve to walk in faith, not fear. Help me to view each challenge through the lens of Your love, knowing that You are working all things for my good. May my heart find rest in You, as I surrender every anxious thought and find refuge in Your loving care.

In Jesus' name, I pray, Amen.

Prayer 9: Be Still and Know (Psalm 46:10)

Merciful Savior, in accordance with Psalm 46:10, "Be still, and know that I am God," I seek Your peace in the midst of my anxiety. In a world that often feels chaotic and overwhelming, teach me to find moments of stillness to connect with You. In these quiet moments, remind me of Your sovereignty and power, reassuring me that You are in control of all things.

In the stillness, help me to lay down my burdens at Your feet. Let Your peace, which surpasses all understanding, fill my heart and mind. In times of worry and stress, may I find comfort in Your presence, knowing that You are God, and that You are with me.

Grant me the grace to trust in Your loving care and provision. As I navigate through life's uncertainties, may I be grounded in the knowledge of Your love and faithfulness. May Your peace reign in my heart, guiding me through each day with confidence and hope in Your unfailing love.

In Jesus' name, I pray, Amen.

Prayer 10: Be Anxious for Nothing (Philippians 4:6-7)

Heavenly Father, in line with Philippians 4:6-7, which encourages us to be anxious for nothing but in everything by prayer and supplication with thanksgiving to make our requests known to You, I bring my anxieties and fears before You. In a world filled with uncertainty and stress, help me to lay down every worry at Your feet and to trust in Your providential care. May the peace that surpasses all understanding guard my heart and mind in Christ Jesus.

In moments of anxiety, remind me of Your constant presence and unfailing love. Let me find solace in Your Word, drawing strength from Your promises that never fail. Teach me to view life's challenges through the lens of faith, not fear, knowing that You are working all things for my good and Your glory.

Grant me the serenity to accept the things I cannot change, the courage to change the things I can, and the wisdom to know the difference. In every anxious moment, may I lean on Your strength and find peace in Your unchanging character. Let my life be a testament to Your grace and a reflection of Your peace.

In Jesus' name, I pray, Amen.

Prayer 11: God of All Comfort (2 Corinthians 1:3-4)

Dear Lord, as the God of all comfort described in 2 Corinthians 1:3-4, I seek Your solace in times of anxiety and stress. When my thoughts are overwhelmed, and my heart is heavy, I turn to You, the source of all comfort and peace. Help me to cast my cares upon You, knowing that You care for me deeply and are always ready to give me the strength I need.

In the midst of my anxieties, guide me to find rest in Your presence. Teach me to trust in Your timing and Your perfect plan for my life. May I find the courage to face each day, not with worry and apprehension, but with a heart full of gratitude and hope, knowing that You are by my side.

Let Your peace, which transcends human understanding, permeate my being. Calm my anxious mind and fill my heart with Your love. In every situation, help me to remember that I am never alone, for You are with me, comforting and guiding me through every storm.

In Jesus' name, I pray,

Amen.

Prayer 12: The Peace of Christ (John 14:27)

Merciful Savior, in harmony with John 14:27, where You offer peace not as the world gives, I turn to You in my struggle with anxiety. In a world where peace can be elusive, I cling to Your promise of divine peace, a peace that remains steady even in life's tumultuous moments. Guard my heart from the anxieties of this world, and grant me the peace that only You can provide.

Help me to anchor my heart in the truth of Your Word. In times of worry, let me remember that You have overcome the world, and in You, I find the strength to face each challenge. Teach me to quiet my mind and to listen for Your gentle whisper of reassurance and guidance.

May Your peace rule in my heart, keeping me from being overwhelmed by anxiety. Help me to rest in the knowledge that You are in control and that Your plans for me are for good. Let the peace of Christ reign in my life, guiding my thoughts and actions as I navigate through each day.

In Jesus' name, I pray,

Amen.

Personal notes:

_____

_____

_____

_____

_____

_____

_____

_____

_____

Prayers for Strength

In times of weakness and challenges, you can find strength in God's promises and His unwavering support. **Isaiah 41:10** assures you, "***So do not fear, for I am with you; do not be dismayed, for I am your God. I will strengthen you and help you; I will uphold you with my righteous right hand***." This verse reminds you that God's strength is always available to you, offering you courage and support in every situation. By relying on God's power and presence, you can overcome obstacles and face life's difficulties with confidence and resilience.

Prayer 1: Guided by His Light

Dear Lord, As taught in Philippians 4:13, "I can do all things through Christ who strengthens me." Lord, I acknowledge my weakness, but I find my strength in you.

I pray that you fill me with your divine power, granting me the strength needed to overcome the challenges before me. May I accomplish all things through your grace and strength.

In Jesus' name, I pray, Amen.

Prayer 2: Anchored in His Power

Dear Father,

Your Word reminds us in 2 Corinthians 12:9 that your grace is sufficient for us, for your power is made perfect in weakness. Lord, I acknowledge my weakness and turn to your power.

Allow me to be anchored in your strength, knowing that when I am weak, I am strong in you. May your grace and power accompany me in all circumstances.

In Jesus' name, I pray, Amen.

Prayer 3: Empowered by Faith

Dear Father,

Your Word reminds us in 2 Corinthians 12:9 that your grace is sufficient for us, for your power is made perfect in weakness. Lord, I acknowledge my weakness and turn to your power.

Allow me to be anchored in your strength, knowing that when I am weak, I am strong in you. May your grace and power accompany me in all circumstances.

In Jesus' name, I pray, Amen.

Prayer 4: Renewed by His Might

Heavenly Father ,

As it is written in Isaiah 40:31, "But those who trust in the Lord shall renew their strength." Lord, I come to you seeking a renewal of my strength.

Grant me the vigor and determination needed to face each day with confidence. May I lean on your steadfast strength to overcome trials.

In Jesus' name, I pray,

Amen.

Prayer 5: Empowered by Divine Strength

Dear Lord,

As taught in Philippians 4:13, "I can do all things through Christ who strengthens me." Lord, I acknowledge my weakness, but I find my strength in you.

I pray that you fill me with your divine power, granting me the strength needed to overcome the challenges before me. May I accomplish all things through your grace and strength.

In Jesus' name, I pray,

Amen.

Prayer 6: Tranquility in Turmoil (John 14:27)

Lord Jesus, as You assured in John 14:27, "Peace I leave with you; my peace I give you," I come seeking solace in the midst of my anxiety. In this world of constant change and uncertainty, grant me the tranquility that only Your presence can provide. Calm my restless heart and quiet my worried mind with the assurance of Your unfailing love and peace.

Help me to trust in Your care and to lay down my burdens at Your feet. In every anxious thought and concern, remind me that You are sovereign and in control. May Your peace, which surpasses all understanding, guard my heart and mind, providing comfort and hope in every moment.

In Jesus' name, I pray,

Amen.

Prayer 7: Strength in Weakness (2 Corinthians 12:9-10)

Heavenly Father, as stated in 2 Corinthians 12:9-10, Your grace is sufficient for me, for Your power is made perfect in weakness. In times when I feel overwhelmed and inadequate, remind me of Your endless grace and the strength that You provide. Help me to embrace my weaknesses as opportunities for Your power to shine through me.

In moments of doubt and exhaustion, renew my spirit with Your energy. Let me find resilience in Your unfailing love, knowing that with You, I can face any challenge. Empower me to persevere through trials, standing steadfast in faith and confident in Your sovereign might.

Grant me the courage to move forward, trusting in Your guidance and provision. May my life be a testament to Your strength working in and through me. Let every obstacle I encounter be an occasion for me to witness Your power and grace at work.

In Jesus' name, I pray,

Amen.

Prayer 8: The Joy of the Lord is My Strength (Nehemiah 8:10)

Lord God, echoing Nehemiah 8:10, I seek the joy of the Lord as my strength. In times of weariness and uncertainty, fill my heart with the joy that comes from knowing You. Let this joy be the source of my strength, uplifting my spirit and enabling me to overcome life's challenges.

Remind me that true joy and strength are found in Your presence and in Your promises. Help me to focus on the blessings You have given me and to rejoice in Your constant faithfulness. May this joy not depend on my circumstances but on the unchanging nature of Your love and grace.

As I walk through each day, let Your joy be my strength, guiding me through difficulties and filling me with peace. May my heart be light and my spirit resilient, as I trust in You and find strength in the joy You provide.

In Jesus' name, I pray

Amen.

Prayer 9: God is My Strength and Shield (Psalm 28:7)

Merciful Savior, inspired by Psalm 28:7, where it is said that You are my strength and my shield, I come to You seeking fortitude and protection. In the face of life's battles and burdens, be my strength, sustaining me when I am weak. Be also my shield, protecting me from the arrows of adversity and doubt.

Help me to trust in Your might and to rely on Your protection. Strengthen my faith in Your unwavering support and guide me with Your wise counsel. In times of vulnerability, remind me that You are my refuge, my fortress against the trials of this world.

May I draw courage and strength from Your presence, finding solace and security in Your loving arms. Let me face each day with confidence, knowing that You are by my side, empowering and defending me in every challenge.

In Jesus' name, I pray

Amen.

Prayer 10: Renewed Strength (Isaiah 40:31)

Heavenly Father, as declared in Isaiah 40:31, "those who hope in the Lord will renew their strength," I come to You in a time of weariness. In moments when my energy fails and my spirit feels weak, I seek the renewal that comes from placing my hope and trust in You. Grant me the strength to rise above my challenges, as the eagles soar above the storm, knowing that my strength is renewed in Your presence.

In times of hardship and exhaustion, guide me to find rest in Your loving arms. Help me to remember that Your power is made perfect in my weakness. May I learn to lean not on my own understanding but to draw strength from Your endless well of grace and mercy.

Empower me to face each day with confidence and perseverance, anchored in the knowledge that You are with me, upholding me with Your righteous right hand. Let me find joy in the journey, strength in the struggle, and peace in Your promises, as I walk in the assurance of Your unwavering support.

In Jesus' name, I pray, Amen.

Prayer 11: The Lord is My Rock (Psalm 18:2)

Lord God, as Psalm 18:2 proclaims, "The Lord is my rock, my fortress, and my deliverer," I seek Your strength in times of uncertainty and challenge. In the midst of life's storms, be my steadfast rock, providing a firm foundation on which I can stand. Be my fortress, where I can find shelter and safety, and my deliverer, rescuing me from the trials that surround me.

In the face of adversity, remind me of Your unchanging nature and Your mighty power. Strengthen my resolve to face each challenge with courage and grace. Help me to trust in Your protection and guidance, knowing that You are my shield and my strength.

May I walk with confidence, knowing that You are my support in every circumstance. Let Your strength be my comfort and Your wisdom my guide. In every moment of weakness, let me find strength in Your presence, secure in the knowledge that You are my rock and my fortress.

In Jesus' name, I pray,

Amen.

Prayer 12: Strength in the Lord (Ephesians 6:10)

Merciful Savior, echoing Ephesians 6:10, "Be strong in the Lord and in his mighty power," I turn to You for strength in my journey. When the road ahead seems daunting and my own strength insufficient, remind me that my true strength comes from You. Equip me with Your armor so that I may stand strong against the challenges and temptations of life.

In my moments of doubt and fear, bolster my spirit with Your power. Teach me to rely on Your strength, not my own, finding courage and resilience in Your unending love and grace. May I face each obstacle with faith, knowing that You are beside me, empowering me to overcome.

Guide me to walk in Your ways, Lord, drawing strength from Your word and comfort in Your presence. As I navigate through life's ups and downs, let me be a witness to Your strength and faithfulness. May my life reflect Your power and grace, inspiring others to find their strength in You.

In Jesus' name, I pray,

Amen.

Personal notes:

_____

_____

_____

_____

_____

_____

_____

_____

_____

_____

_____

_____

_____

_____

_____

_____

Prayers for Forgiveness

Forgiveness is crucial for your spiritual and emotional well-being, as it frees you from the burden of resentment and allows you to experience peace and healing. In **Ephesians 4:32**, the Bible instructs, "**Be kind and compassionate to one another, forgiving each other, just as in Christ God forgave you.**" This verse emphasizes the importance of forgiving others as you have been forgiven by God. By practicing forgiveness, you reflect God's love and mercy, fostering healthier relationships and a more harmonious life.

Prayer 1: A Heart of Forgiveness (Matthew 6:14-15)

Heavenly Father, in accordance with Matthew 6:14-15, which teaches us to forgive others so that we may be forgiven, I seek Your strength to forgive those who have wronged me. Help me to let go of bitterness and anger, replacing them with compassion and understanding. Let my heart reflect Your grace and mercy.

Guide me in the path of forgiveness, so I may experience the freedom and peace it brings. Teach me to forgive as freely as You have forgiven me. May my actions and words be a testament to the transformative power of Your love and forgiveness in my life.

In Jesus' name, I pray

Amen.

Prayer 2: Renewed by Grace (Ephesians 4:32)

Dear Lord, as Ephesians 4:32 urges us to be kind and compassionate to one another, forgiving each other just as in Christ, God forgave us, I ask for a heart that is open to forgiveness. In moments of hurt and misunderstanding, grant me the grace to forgive, remembering the immense forgiveness I have received through Christ.

Help me to embrace forgiveness as a pathway to healing and reconciliation. May my actions embody the kindness and forgiveness You have shown me, creating a ripple of grace in my relationships and interactions with others.

In Jesus' name, I pray

Amen.

Prayer 3: The Power of Mercy (Luke 6:37)

Merciful Savior, guided by Luke 6:37, "Forgive, and you will be forgiven," I come to You seeking the courage to forgive and to let go of past hurts. In the journey towards forgiveness, help me to understand the depth of Your mercy and to extend that mercy to others.

Teach me to be compassionate and forgiving, breaking the chains of resentment and bitterness. As I walk in forgiveness, let my life be a reflection of Your love and an example of Your boundless mercy to those around me.

In Jesus' name, I pray, Amen.

Prayer 4: Forgive and Be Forgiven (Luke 6:37)

Heavenly Father, as You teach in Luke 6:37, "Forgive, and you will be forgiven," I come before You seeking the grace to forgive others. Help me release any harbored bitterness and resentment, and fill my heart with compassion and understanding. May I remember the forgiveness I have received in Christ, and extend that same forgiveness to those who have wronged me.

In forgiving others, I recognize my own need for Your forgiveness. Cleanse my heart, Lord, and renew a right spirit within me. Teach me to walk in love and forgiveness, reflecting Your mercy and grace in my daily interactions.

In Jesus' name, I pray

Amen.

Prayer 5: A Clean Heart (Psalm 51:10)

Dear Lord, inspired by Psalm 51:10, "Create in me a clean heart, O God, and renew a right spirit within me," I ask for Your forgiveness for my transgressions. Guide me in the path of repentance and help me to turn away from my sinful ways. Grant me a heart that seeks after You and desires to do Your will.

Forgive me, Father, and wash away my iniquities. May Your love and grace renew my spirit and guide me back to You. Help me to live in the freedom of Your forgiveness, striving each day to be more like Christ.

In Jesus' name, I pray

Amen.

Prayer 6: Grace Abounds (Romans 5:20)

Merciful Savior, as Romans 5:20 declares, "Where sin increased, grace abounded all the more," I come to You acknowledging my faults and failures. In moments of weakness and failure, remind me of Your abundant grace and the forgiveness that is available through Jesus Christ. Let Your grace cover my mistakes and lead me to repentance.

Help me, Lord, to accept Your forgiveness and to forgive myself. Teach me to grow from my mistakes and to walk in the newness of life that You offer. May Your grace empower me to overcome sin and to live a life that honors You.

In Jesus' name, I pray, Amen.

Prayer 7: Mercy Like Rain (Lamentations 3:22-23)

Heavenly Father, inspired by Lamentations 3:22-23, "Because of the Lord's great love we are not consumed, for his compassions never fail," I seek Your forgiveness for my shortcomings and failings. Your mercies are new every morning, and in this, I find hope and solace. Help me to understand the depth of Your forgiveness, that I may truly repent and turn back to You with a contrite heart.

In moments of weakness, when I stumble and fall, remind me of Your unfailing love and grace. Teach me to extend the same forgiveness to others, breaking the cycle of hurt and bitterness. May Your love and mercy guide my actions and reactions, reflecting the forgiveness and grace that I have received from You.

Let my life be a testimony to Your endless mercy. As the rain renews the earth, may Your forgiveness renew my spirit. Create in me a clean heart, O God, and renew a steadfast spirit within me. Help me to live each day in the light of Your forgiveness, walking in love and grace.

In Jesus' name, I pray, Amen.

Prayer 8: The Path of Forgiveness (Psalm 32:1-2)

Dear Lord, as Psalm 32:1-2 declares, "Blessed is the one whose transgressions are forgiven, whose sins are covered," I come to You acknowledging my need for Your forgiveness. I confess my sins, knowing that You are faithful and just to forgive. Guide me on the path of repentance, where I can experience the joy and freedom that comes from being forgiven.

Grant me the humility to seek forgiveness from those I have wronged. As You have forgiven me, so let me forgive others. Help me to release any grudges or feelings of resentment, replacing them with love and understanding.

May my heart be light, free from the burden of guilt and shame. Strengthen me to resist temptation and to live a life that is pleasing to You. Teach me to walk in Your ways, embracing the fullness of Your forgiveness and sharing it with others.

In Jesus' name, I pray, Amen.

Prayer 9: A New Creation in Christ (2 Corinthians 5:17)

Merciful Savior, based on 2 Corinthians 5:17, "Therefore, if anyone is in Christ, the new creation has come: The old has gone, the new is here!" I seek Your transformative forgiveness. In Christ, I am a new creation; my past mistakes are gone, and a new life lies before me. Help me to embrace this new identity, leaving behind the old ways and stepping forward into the life You have planned for me.

Forgive me for the times I've failed to live up to Your expectations. In Your mercy, restore and renew my spirit. Teach me to walk in the light of Your love, growing daily in Your likeness, and reflecting Your grace and truth in my actions.

Empower me to live as a new creation, not bound by past mistakes but liberated through Your forgiveness. May I extend this grace to others, living out the love and forgiveness that You have so freely given me. Let my life be a shining example of Your redeeming work, drawing others to Your mercy and love.

In Jesus' name, I pray, Amen.

Prayer 10: Lead Us in Your Forgiveness (Matthew 6:12)

Heavenly Father, as You teach us in Matthew 6:12 to pray, "Forgive us our debts, as we also have forgiven our debtors," I come to You seeking the strength to forgive and be forgiven. In moments where resentment and anger cloud my judgment, grant me the grace to let go and embrace the healing power of forgiveness. May I remember the vastness of Your mercy towards me and extend that same compassion to others.

In seeking Your forgiveness, I acknowledge my own failings and the times I have fallen short. Cleanse my heart of any malice and bitterness, and renew a right spirit within me. Let me be a vessel of Your peace and forgiveness, showing others the path to reconciliation through Your love.

Strengthen my resolve to walk in Your ways, Lord. May my life reflect the forgiveness I have received through Christ, and may I be quick to forgive, just as You have forgiven me. Teach me to live each day with a heart that is open to both giving and receiving forgiveness.

In Jesus' name, I pray, Amen.

Prayer 11: Restored by Mercy (Psalm 51:1-2)

Dear Lord, echoing the heartfelt plea of Psalm 51:1-2, "Have mercy on me, O God, according to your unfailing love," I seek Your forgiveness for my transgressions. Wash me clean from my iniquity and cleanse me from my sin. In moments of regret and guilt, remind me of Your boundless love and readiness to forgive.

As I strive to live a life pleasing to You, guide me in the path of righteousness. Help me to turn away from my sinful ways and to embrace the transformative power of Your mercy. May my heart be open to receive Your grace and to learn from my mistakes.

May the knowledge of Your mercy bring comfort and hope to my soul. Create in me a clean heart, O God, and renew a right spirit within me. Let my life be a reflection of Your grace and a testimony to the redemptive power of Your forgiveness.

In Jesus' name, I pray, Amen.

Prayer 12: Grace Upon Grace (John 1:16)

Merciful Savior, as John 1:16 declares, "From his fullness we have all received, grace upon grace," I come to You acknowledging my need for Your grace and forgiveness. In times of failure and weakness, help me to remember that Your grace is sufficient for all my shortcomings. Guide me to seek Your forgiveness with a humble and repentant heart.

Teach me, Lord, to extend grace to those around me. Just as You have lavishly bestowed Your grace upon me, may I generously share that grace with others. Let my life be marked by a spirit of forgiveness, understanding, and compassion, mirroring the grace I have received.

May Your grace inspire me to grow and change, leaving behind the old self and stepping into the new life You have prepared for me. Help me to forgive as I have been forgiven, to love as I have been loved, and to extend grace as I have been graced by You.

In Jesus' name, I pray

Amen.

Personal notes:

_____

_____

_____

_____

_____

_____

_____

_____

_____

Prayers for Prosperity

Prosperity is significant as it allows you to not only enjoy the fruits of your labor but also to be a blessing to others. In **Jeremiah 29:11**, the Bible says, "*For I know the plans I have for you, declares the Lord, plans to prosper you and not to harm you, plans to give you hope and a future.*" This verse highlights that God's intention is for you to thrive and flourish. When you experience prosperity, you are in a better position to help those in need, contribute to your community, and fulfill the purpose God has for your life.

Prayer 1: Blessings of Abundance (Philippians 4:19)

Heavenly Father, according to Philippians 4:19, "And my God will meet all your needs according to the riches of his glory in Christ Jesus," I pray for Your blessings of prosperity and abundance. Guide me in my endeavors, and provide me with the wisdom and opportunities to achieve financial stability and success. Help me to use these blessings wisely, for the benefit of not just myself but also those around me.

In seeking prosperity, let me not lose sight of the true wealth found in Your love and salvation. May my pursuit of success be grounded in gratitude and generosity, reflecting Your goodness and provision in every aspect of my life.

In Jesus' name, I pray, Amen.

Prayer 2: Plans for Prosperity (Jeremiah 29:11)

Lord, as declared in Jeremiah 29:11, "For I know the plans I have for you, declares the Lord, plans for welfare and not for evil, to give you a future and a hope," I entrust my aspirations and goals to Your loving care. Lead me on the path of prosperity that aligns with Your will, opening doors that no one can shut and blessing my efforts with Your favor and success.

Teach me to balance ambition with humility, and hard work with trust in Your timing. May my achievements and growth always honor You, and may I never forget to give thanks for every blessing and breakthrough on my journey.

In Jesus' name, I pray, Amen.

Prayer 3: Harvest of Blessings (2 Corinthians 9:10)

Merciful Savior, inspired by 2 Corinthians 9:10, "Now he who supplies seed to the sower and bread for food will also supply and increase your store of seed and will enlarge the harvest of your righteousness," I ask for Your blessings upon my work and efforts. Grant me the resources and abilities to prosper and succeed. Let my work not only bring personal gain but also be a source of blessing to others.

Help me to sow seeds of diligence, integrity, and kindness in my pursuits, trusting that You will bring a fruitful harvest. In every success, may I recognize and celebrate Your hand at work, sharing my blessings generously with those in need.

In Jesus' name, I pray, Amen.

Prayer 4: Paths of Prosperity (Psalm 23:1)

Heavenly Father, as Psalm 23:1 reminds us, "The Lord is my shepherd; I shall not want," I pray for Your guidance on the paths of prosperity. Lead me in Your wisdom to opportunities that foster growth and success.

Bless my endeavors with Your favor, and provide the resources and insights needed to thrive in my personal and professional life.

Help me to trust in Your provision, knowing that You care for all my needs. May my journey of prosperity be a reflection of Your grace and abundance, enabling me to share Your blessings with others and glorify Your name in all that I do.

In Jesus' name, I pray,

Amen.

Prayer 5: Fruitful Endeavors (Jeremiah 17:7-8)

Lord, as declared in Jeremiah 17:7-8, "Blessed is the man who trusts in the Lord," I place my trust in You for prosperity in all my endeavors. Let my efforts be like a tree planted by the water, yielding fruit in season. Grant me the perseverance and resilience to flourish even in challenging times, drawing strength and nourishment from Your unending love.

Bless the work of my hands, and let my actions reflect Your wisdom and integrity. In my pursuit of success, keep my heart aligned with Your purpose, using the fruits of my labor to bless others and to contribute positively to my community.

In Jesus' name, I pray,

Amen.

Prayer 6: Abundance in God's Timing (Ecclesiastes 3:1-2)

Merciful Savior, as Ecclesiastes 3:1-2 teaches us, "To everything there is a season," I pray for prosperity in Your perfect timing. Help me to understand the seasons of my life and to trust in Your impeccable plan for my growth and success. Provide me with the patience and faith to wait for the harvest You have prepared for me.

Guide me in making wise decisions that align with Your will, and bless my efforts with abundance. Let my journey towards prosperity be a testament to Your faithfulness, teaching me to be grateful in all circumstances and generous with the blessings You bestow.

In Jesus' name, I pray,

Amen.

Prayer 7: Prosper in All Things (3 John 1:2)

Heavenly Father, as expressed in 3 John 1:2, where it is written, "I pray that you may prosper in all things and be in health, just as your soul prospers," I seek Your blessing on my life's endeavors. Grant me the wisdom to make wise choices that lead to prosperity and success. Help me to balance hard work with faith in Your providence, knowing that all good things come from You.

Open doors of opportunity and guide my steps on the path to financial stability and abundance. Bless my efforts so that I may not only provide for my needs and those of my family but also extend generosity to others. Let my life be a testament to Your faithfulness and a reflection of Your abundant blessings.

I pray for health in body and soul, understanding that true prosperity encompasses more than material wealth. May my journey be marked by growth, contentment, and a spirit of gratitude for all that You have given me. In every endeavor, let me honor You and serve as a witness to Your goodness.

In Jesus' name, I pray,

Amen.

Prayer 8: Guided to Abundance (Matthew 6:33)

Merciful Savior, in line with Matthew 6:33, "But seek first his kingdom and his righteousness, and all these things will be given to you as well," I entrust my desires for prosperity to You. Help me to prioritize my spiritual growth and service to others, trusting that in doing so, my material needs will be met according to Your perfect plan.

Provide me with the discernment to recognize the opportunities You place before me and the courage to seize them. Bless my endeavors with success, not just for my gain but for the betterment of those around me and for the advancement of Your kingdom. Teach me to use the resources You provide wisely and generously.

May my pursuit of prosperity be accompanied by an unwavering commitment to Your principles and love. Let my actions reflect my faith, and may my journey be a testament to Your provision and blessing. In all things, let me glorify You and serve as a beacon of Your grace and abundance.

In Jesus' name, I pray,

Amen.

Prayer 9: Fruitful in Labor (Psalm 1:3)

Lord God, drawing inspiration from Psalm 1:3, "He is like a tree planted by streams of water, which yields its fruit in season," I ask for Your blessing on my work and ventures. May my efforts be rooted in Your wisdom, yielding success and growth. Guide me to be diligent and resourceful, flourishing like a tree by the water, nourished by Your love and grace.

Grant me the creativity and strength to overcome challenges and to find joy in my labor. Let my work not only bring prosperity but also fulfillment and purpose. May each task I undertake be an opportunity to showcase Your glory and to build a legacy that honors You.

Bless me with a spirit of collaboration and community, understanding that prosperity grows from shared efforts and mutual support. Help me to uplift others in their endeavors, recognizing that together, we can achieve greater success and reflect the richness of Your kingdom.

In Jesus' name, I pray

Amen.

Prayer 10: Blessings of Prosperity (Proverbs 10:22)

Heavenly Father, guided by Proverbs 10:22, which says, "The blessing of the Lord brings wealth, without painful toil for it," I seek Your divine favor in my life. Bless my endeavors, work, and plans with the richness of Your grace. May Your blessings bring prosperity that enriches not only my life but also those around me, without the burden of sorrow or strife.

Grant me wisdom to manage the resources You provide wisely and generously. Help me to recognize the opportunities You place before me and to use them for the betterment of my family, community, and Your kingdom. May my actions and decisions reflect a heart aligned with Your will, bringing honor and glory to Your name.

In every step of my journey towards prosperity, keep me humble and grateful. Let me never forget that all I have and all I achieve is through Your grace and love. May my life be a testimony of Your abundant provision and a beacon of hope to others.

In Jesus' name, I pray,

Amen.

Prayer 11: Walking in Abundance (2 Corinthians 9:8)

Lord, as stated in 2 Corinthians 9:8, "And God is able to bless you abundantly, so that in all things at all times, having all that you need, you will abound in every good work," I ask for Your abundant blessings in my life. Provide me with the means to achieve not just financial success but also richness in spirit and character. Help me to excel in my work and contributions, making a positive impact on those around me.

Empower me to be a channel of Your blessings, using the prosperity You grant me to help and uplift others. Instill in me a spirit of generosity, that I may share freely and joyfully. May the abundance You provide extend beyond material wealth to touch lives and bring glory to Your kingdom.

Keep me grounded in Your teachings, Lord, reminding me that true prosperity comes from a life lived in accordance with Your word. Let my journey towards abundance be filled with faith, love, and service, guided always by Your eternal wisdom.

In Jesus' name, I pray

Amen.

Prayer 12: Harvest of Blessings (Philippians 4:19)

Merciful Savior, in harmony with Philippians 4:19, "And my God will meet all your needs according to the riches of his glory in Christ Jesus," I come before You with open hands and heart. Bless my efforts and endeavors so that I may experience a harvest of blessings. May my work and dedication yield prosperity that reflects Your goodness and provides for both my needs and the needs of others.

Guide me in using the talents and abilities You have bestowed upon me to their fullest potential. Help me to see the paths You have laid out for me and to walk them with confidence and faith. May the success I achieve bear witness to Your gracious provision and inspire gratitude and generosity in my heart and in the hearts of others.

Let my pursuit of prosperity always be tempered with an understanding of Your will and purpose for my life. May the prosperity I seek align with Your plans for me, contributing to a life of service, joy, and fulfillment in Your presence.

In Jesus' name, I pray,

Amen.

Personal notes:

_____

_____

_____

_____

_____

_____

_____

_____

_____

_____

_____

_____

_____

_____

_____

_____

_____

Prayers for Self-Love & Loving Others

Prayers for self-love and loving others are essential for nurturing a compassionate heart and maintaining healthy relationships. In **Matthew 22:39**, Jesus commands, **"*You shall love your neighbor as yourself.*"** This verse underscores the importance of loving yourself in order to genuinely love others. By praying for self-love, you ask God to help you see your worth through His eyes and embrace His unconditional love. Simultaneously, praying for the ability to love others ensures that you reflect God's love in your interactions, fostering kindness, empathy, and unity.

Prayer 1: Created in His Image (Genesis 1:27)

Heavenly Father, as declared in Genesis 1:27, "So God created mankind in his own image," I come to You seeking the grace to love and accept myself as Your creation. Help me to see the beauty and worth that You have instilled in me. Teach me to appreciate my uniqueness and to embrace the person You have designed me to be.

Guide me in nurturing self-love that reflects the love You have for me. Banish any thoughts of self-doubt or insecurity, replacing them with the confidence that comes from knowing I am fearfully and wonderfully made by You. Let me walk in the assurance of Your love and acceptance.

In Jesus' name, I pray, Amen.

Prayer 2: Temple of the Holy Spirit (1 Corinthians 6:19-20)

Lord, as reminded in 1 Corinthians 6:19-20, "Your body is a temple of the Holy Spirit," I pray for the strength to honor and love myself as Your temple. Help me to care for my body, mind, and soul with respect and tenderness, recognizing them as gifts from You. May I treat myself with the same compassion and care that I offer to others.

Empower me to respect my limitations and to celebrate my strengths. In moments of self-criticism or doubt, remind me that I am valued and loved by You. Let my self-love be an expression of gratitude for Your miraculous creation.

In Jesus' name, I pray, Amen.

Prayer 3: Love Yourself as Your Neighbor (Mark 12:31)

Merciful Savior, inspired by Mark 12:31, "Love your neighbor as yourself," I seek the wisdom to extend the same love and kindness to myself that I show to others. Help me to recognize my worth and to treat myself with gentleness and understanding. Teach me to value my own needs and to find joy and fulfillment in my journey with You.

In times of self-doubt or harsh self-judgment, guide me back to Your truth and love. Remind me that I am deserving of love and care, not because of what I do, but because I am Yours. May my journey of self-love be a testament to Your grace and compassion in my life.

In Jesus' name, I pray, Amen.

Prayer 4: Fearfully and Wonderfully Made (Psalm 139:14)

Heavenly Father, guided by Psalm 139:14, "I praise you because I am fearfully and wonderfully made," I seek to embrace the unique person You have created me to be. Help me to see myself with the eyes of love and acceptance, recognizing the beauty and worth You have placed within me. Teach me to value myself and to understand that I am a precious creation in Your sight.

In moments of self-doubt and criticism, remind me of Your unconditional love. Grant me the strength to overcome negative thoughts and to replace them with Your truths. Let me find comfort and confidence in knowing that I am created in Your image, destined for a purpose only I can fulfill.

May my journey of self-love be rooted in Your love for me. Help me to treat myself with kindness and compassion, reflecting the love You have shown me. In loving myself, let me be a mirror of Your grace, shining Your light and love to those around me.

In Jesus' name, I pray, Amen.

Prayer 5: A Temple of the Holy Spirit (1 Corinthians 6:19-20)

Merciful Savior, in line with 1 Corinthians 6:19-20, "Your body is a temple of the Holy Spirit," I ask for Your help in loving and caring for myself as Your precious dwelling. Let me honor my body and mind, recognizing them as sacred gifts entrusted to me. May I cultivate self-love that respects and cherishes my whole being as a temple of Your Spirit.

Help me to nurture my health, well-being, and personal growth, understanding that self-care honors You. Teach me to balance my life in a way that strengthens me physically, emotionally, and spiritually. In moments of neglect or harsh judgment, gently guide me back to a path of self-love and care.

Through self-love, may I glorify You in my body and spirit. Let this journey of self-compassion lead me closer to You, showing gratitude for the life You have given me. Help me to radiate the love and respect I have for myself in my interactions with others, demonstrating the transformative power of Your love in my life.

In Jesus' name, I pray, Amen.

Prayer 6: Love One Another (John 13:34)

Heavenly Father, as Jesus taught us in John 13:34, "Love one another. As I have loved you, so you must love one another," I pray for a heart that mirrors this divine command. Instill in me the capacity to love others unconditionally, seeing them through Your eyes of grace and compassion. Help me to understand and embrace our shared humanity, extending kindness and empathy to all.

Guide my actions and words to be a reflection of Your love. In moments of conflict or misunderstanding, grant me the wisdom to respond with patience and understanding. May my life be a testament to Your enduring love, fostering unity and peace in my interactions with others.

In Jesus' name, I pray,

Amen.

Prayer 7: The Greatest Commandment (Matthew 22:39)

Lord, in accordance with Matthew 22:39, "Love your neighbor as yourself," I seek Your guidance in loving others as fervently and genuinely as I care for myself. Open my heart to the needs and feelings of those around me. Let me be a source of comfort and support, embodying the love You have called us to share.

Help me to practice empathy and kindness in all my relationships. Remind me to be patient, forgiving, and selfless, reflecting Your love in every interaction. Let my life be an example of Your command to love, breaking down barriers and building bridges of understanding and compassion.

In Jesus' name, I pray,

Amen.

Prayer 8: Bound in Perfect Unity (Colossians 3:14)

Merciful Savior, as Colossians 3:14 urges, "And over all these virtues put on love, which binds them all together in perfect unity," I pray for the strength to embody this perfect love. Help me to cultivate a heart that is patient, kind, and forgiving, actively seeking the good of others above my own. Let my life be a channel of Your peace and love, uniting those around me.

Teach me to embrace diversity and to find strength in our differences. May my actions be guided by Your unwavering love, fostering harmony and understanding in my community and beyond. Through love, let me contribute to a world bound in unity, reflecting the beauty of Your creation.

In Jesus' name, I pray,

Amen.

Prayer 9: Love Thy Neighbor (Matthew 22:39)

Heavenly Father, as You command in Matthew 22:39, "Love your neighbor as yourself," I ask for Your help to truly live out this teaching. Fill my heart with unconditional love for others, just as You love each of us. Help me to see beyond differences and to understand the value and worth of every individual.

In my interactions, guide me to act with kindness, patience, and empathy. Let my words and actions be a reflection of Your love and grace. Teach me to listen with an open heart, to speak with gentleness, and to act with compassion in every situation.

May my life be a testament to the love I have for my neighbors. Through my example, let others feel Your presence and be inspired to share love in their own communities. May this ripple of love create a wave of kindness and understanding across the world.

In Jesus' name, I pray,

Amen.

Prayer 10: A New Commandment (John 13:34)

Lord Jesus, following Your new commandment in John 13:34, "Love one another. As I have loved you, so you must love one another," I pray for the strength to embody this profound love. Help me to extend grace and forgiveness, to understand, and to be present for others as You are for me.

In moments of challenge or frustration, remind me to respond with love. Teach me to set aside judgment and to approach each person with compassion and empathy. Let me be a source of support, encouragement, and understanding, showing Your love in my everyday actions.

Inspire me to build bridges of love and reconciliation in my community. May my words and deeds foster unity and peace, drawing others closer to You. Through loving others, let me be a beacon of Your light and hope in this world.

In Jesus' name, I pray,

Amen.

Prayer 11: The Greatest of These (1 Corinthians 13:13)

Merciful Savior, in line with 1 Corinthians 13:13, "And now these three remain: faith, hope, and love. But the greatest of these is love," I seek to embody the greatest virtue of all. Help me to love others not just in words but in actions and truth. May my life be a living expression of the love You have shown to me.

Let me approach each day with a heart full of love for those around me. Whether in small acts of kindness or significant gestures of support, let my love be genuine and impactful. Teach me to love without expectation, to give without seeking return, and to uplift those in need.

In my journey of loving others, guide me to always reflect Your love and compassion. Let my actions bring light to those in darkness and comfort to those in need. Through my love, may others come to know the depth and breadth of Your love for us all.

In Jesus' name, I pray

Amen.

Personal notes:

_____

_____

_____

_____

_____

_____

_____

_____

_____

_____

_____

_____

_____

_____

_____

_____

Prayers For Faith Restoration

Prayers for faith restoration are very important because they help you reconnect with God's presence and power in your life, especially during times of doubt or spiritual struggle. In **Hebrews 11:6,** the Bible states, "***And without faith it is impossible to please God, because anyone who comes to him must believe that he exists and that he rewards those who earnestly seek him.***" This verse highlights the fundamental role of faith in your relationship with God. By praying for the restoration of your faith, you invite God to renew your trust in His promises, strengthen your spiritual foundation, and guide you through life's challenges with confidence and hope

Prayer 1: Renewed Faith (Isaiah 40:31)

Heavenly Father, as Isaiah 40:31 promises, "Those who hope in the Lord will renew their strength," I come before You seeking the restoration of my faith. In times of doubt and uncertainty, remind me of Your unwavering presence and love. Renew my spirit, Lord, and rekindle the flame of faith within me, that I may trust in You with renewed vigor and hope.

Help me to see Your hand at work in my life and in the world around me. Strengthen my belief in Your promises, and guide me back to a place of deep faith and reliance on You. May my journey of faith be a testament to Your enduring grace and love.

In Jesus' name, I pray, Amen.

Prayer 2: Anchor of the Soul (Hebrews 6:19)

Lord, as Hebrews 6:19 describes, "We have this hope as an anchor for the soul, firm and secure," I ask for Your assistance in restoring my faith. In challenging times, when my faith wavers, anchor me with Your steadfast love and truth. Reaffirm in my heart the hope and assurance that comes from trusting in You.

Guide me through the storms of life, keeping my eyes fixed on You, the author and perfecter of my faith. Strengthen me to overcome doubts, and fill me with the peace that surpasses understanding. Let my faith be anchored in Your word, unwavering and strong.

In Jesus' name, I pray, Amen.

Prayer 3: Walking by Faith (2 Corinthians 5:7)

Merciful Savior, inspired by 2 Corinthians 5:7, "For we live by faith, not by sight," I seek Your guidance in restoring my faith. When the path ahead seems unclear, and my vision clouded by the trials of life, remind me to walk by faith, trusting in Your divine wisdom and timing.

Help me to surrender my doubts and fears to You, embracing faith even when I cannot see the way forward. Strengthen my trust in Your plans, knowing that You work all things for good. May my life reflect a journey of faith, steadily walking with You, guided by Your light and truth.

In Jesus' name, I pray, Amen.

Prayer 4: Revive My Faith (Luke 17:5)

Heavenly Father, in accordance with the plea of the apostles in Luke 17:5, "Increase our faith," I come to You seeking a revival of my faith. In times when my belief wavers and doubts cloud my mind, I ask for Your guiding light to lead me back to a place of strong faith and trust in Your promises. Renew my spirit, Lord, and fill me with the assurance of Your unfailing love and power.

In moments of uncertainty or fear, remind me of the countless ways You have been faithful in the past. Help me to recall the strength found in my faith, and the peace it brings to my soul. Rekindle the flame of belief in my heart, allowing me to witness Your works with a renewed sense of wonder and gratitude.

Let my faith be a beacon of hope not only for myself but for those around me. Strengthen my resolve to trust in You, even when the path is unclear. May my restored faith be a testament to Your grace, leading me to walk in confidence and peace.

In Jesus' name, I pray, Amen.

Prayer 5: Faith as a Mustard Seed (Matthew 17:20)

Lord Jesus, inspired by Your words in Matthew 17:20, "If you have faith as small as a mustard seed," I ask for the renewal of my faith, even if it starts small. Help me to nurture this seed of belief, trusting that it will grow and flourish under Your care. Teach me to find strength in the smallest expressions of faith, and to trust in Your power to work wonders in my life.

Encourage me when I feel my faith faltering, and guide me to seek Your presence and wisdom. Let every challenge be an opportunity to strengthen my trust in You. May I find courage and resilience in the knowledge that my faith, no matter its size, is precious in Your sight.

Grant me the patience to wait for the blooming of this seed of faith. May it grow into a strong, unwavering belief that guides my thoughts and actions. Through this journey, let my growing faith be a source of inspiration and encouragement to others who also seek to deepen their trust in You.

In Jesus' name, I pray, Amen.

Prayer 6: Walking by Faith (2 Corinthians 5:7)

Merciful Savior, echoing the sentiment of 2 Corinthians 5:7, "For we live by faith, not by sight," I seek the restoration of my faith in this journey called life. When the road becomes difficult and my vision is clouded by trials, help me to cling to faith, trusting in Your wisdom and sovereignty. Strengthen my belief in Your goodness and Your plan for my life.

In moments of weakness and doubt, remind me of Your unwavering presence and the power of faith to overcome obstacles. Help me to walk each day with a firm belief in Your word and Your promises, finding comfort in knowing that You are with me every step of the way.

May my renewed faith be a testimony of Your love and faithfulness. Let it shine as a light of hope and guidance, not only in my life but also as an encouragement to others facing their own struggles. Through my faith, may I reflect Your love and grace to the world.

In Jesus' name, I pray, Amen.

Personal notes:

_____

_____

_____

_____

_____

_____

Prayers for Building Faith

Prayers for building faith are essential because they strengthen your relationship with God and equip you to face life's challenges with confidence and resilience. **Romans 10:17** states, "*So then faith comes by hearing, and hearing by the word of God.*" This verse emphasizes that faith is nurtured through engagement with God's Word. By praying for the development of your faith, you ask God to deepen your understanding of His truth, increase your trust in His promises, and guide you in living out your faith daily. This spiritual growth not only fortifies your own life but also enables you to inspire and support others in their faith journeys.

Prayer 1: Foundation of Faith (Matthew 7:24-25)

Heavenly Father, as Jesus taught in Matthew 7:24-25 about building our house on the rock, I pray for Your guidance in building a strong foundation of faith in my life. Help me to ground my beliefs and actions in Your word, that I may stand firm in trials and storms. Teach me to trust in You wholeheartedly, drawing strength and wisdom from Your unchanging truth.

In times of uncertainty or temptation, remind me to turn to You as my solid foundation. Strengthen my resolve to follow Your teachings and to grow in faith each day. May my life reflect the stability and resilience that comes from building my faith upon the rock of Your word and love.

In Jesus' name, I pray

Amen.

Prayer 2: Growing in Faith (2 Thessalonians 1:3)

Lord, as Paul celebrated the growing faith of the Thessalonians in 2 Thessalonians 1:3, I too seek to nurture and expand my faith in You. Inspire me to delve deeper into Your word, to engage in prayer continually, and to seek fellowship that encourages spiritual growth. Let every experience, both challenging and joyful, be an opportunity to develop a stronger, more resilient faith.

May my journey of faith be marked by constant learning and an ever-deepening understanding of Your grace. Help me to apply Your teachings in my daily life, allowing my faith to shine through my actions. Let my growing faith be a beacon to others, inspiring them to seek a closer relationship with You.

In Jesus' name, I pray, Amen.

Prayer 3: Walking by Faith (2 Corinthians 5:7)

Merciful Savior, echoing 2 Corinthians 5:7, "For we live by faith, not by sight," I ask for Your support in strengthening my walk of faith. In a world where uncertainty and skepticism often prevail, help me to keep my eyes fixed on You, trusting in Your promises and guidance. Teach me to walk by faith in every aspect of my life, confident in Your sovereign plan.

In times when my path seems unclear or obstacles arise, bolster my faith to trust in Your timing and purpose. May my journey be a testament to the power of living by faith, showing perseverance, hope, and a deep trust in Your providential care.

In Jesus' name, I pray, Amen.

Prayer 4: Strengthen My Belief (Mark 9:24)

Heavenly Father, echoing the cry of the father in Mark 9:24, "I do believe; help me overcome my unbelief," I ask for Your assistance in strengthening my faith. In moments of doubt or confusion, guide me back to the truth and certainty of Your word. Fill my heart with the conviction of Your promises and the assurance of Your love.

Grant me the courage to trust in You even when the path is unclear. Nurture my faith through every trial and triumph, using them to draw me closer to You. Help me to rely not on my understanding but on Your infinite wisdom and guidance.

May my growing faith be a beacon of hope to those around me. Let it be a testament to Your faithfulness, encouraging others to seek and find comfort in Your loving embrace.

In Jesus' name, I pray, Amen.

Prayer 5: Rooted in Faith (Colossians 2:7)

Lord, as Colossians 2:7 urges, "rooted and built up in him, strengthened in the faith as you were taught," I seek to deepen my faith in You. In a world of shifting sands, let my belief be rooted in the solid ground of Your word. May each day bring a new understanding of Your teachings and a stronger connection to You.

Help me to build my life upon the foundation of Your love and truth. Guide me in applying Your teachings to my daily life, so that my actions may reflect the depth and sincerity of my faith. In moments of uncertainty, remind me that You are my rock and my fortress.

Let my faith be an unwavering anchor in the storms of life. May it grow and flourish, producing fruit that brings glory to Your name. Through this journey of faith, let me be a source of encouragement and strength to others.

In Jesus' name, I pray,

Amen.

Prayer 6: A Journey of Faith (Hebrews 11:1)

Merciful Savior, inspired by Hebrews 11:1, "Now faith is confidence in what we hope for and assurance about what we do not see," I embark on a journey to build and fortify my faith in You. Teach me to trust in Your unseen hand guiding my life, knowing that Your plans for me are good and filled with hope.

In times of hardship or doubt, reinforce my faith with the reminder of Your presence and power. Help me to find strength in the stories of those who walked before me, their lives a testament to the enduring power of faith. Encourage me to persist in prayer and meditation on Your word.

As I grow in faith, let it shape every aspect of my life. May it guide my decisions, influence my relationships, and lead me to act with love and grace. In this journey, may my faith be a living reflection of Your love and a light to those in need of Your hope.

In Jesus' name, I pray,

Amen.

Personal notes:

_____

_____

_____

_____

_____

_____

_____

_____

_____

_____

_____

_____

_____

_____

_____

_____

_____

_____

_____

Prayers for Growing Faith

Prayers for growing faith are important because they help you cultivate a deeper trust in God, enabling you to navigate life's uncertainties with assurance and peace. In **Mark 9:24**, a man seeking Jesus' help cries out, "***I do believe; help me overcome my unbelief!***" This verse highlights the need for ongoing spiritual growth and the desire to strengthen one's faith. By praying for an increase in faith, you invite God to work in your heart, helping you to understand His will, rely on His promises, and act with confidence in His guidance.

Prayer 1: Deepening My Trust (Proverbs 3:5-6)

Heavenly Father, as Proverbs 3:5-6 instructs, "Trust in the Lord with all your heart and lean not on your own understanding," I pray for a deepening of my faith in You. Help me to rely wholeheartedly on Your guidance and to seek Your wisdom in all aspects of my life. Let me embrace Your plans, knowing that they are for my good and Your glory.

In times of uncertainty or challenge, remind me to trust in Your sovereignty. Strengthen my faith when I am overwhelmed by the circumstances around me. Teach me to find peace and confidence in the assurance of Your unfailing love and power.

May my journey of faith be marked by continuous growth and a steadfast commitment to You. Help me to reflect Your love and grace in my actions, becoming a living testament to the strength and peace that comes from trusting in You.

In Jesus' name, I pray, Amen.

Prayer 2: Roots of Faith (Jeremiah 17:7-8)

Lord, inspired by Jeremiah 17:7-8, "Blessed is the one who trusts in the Lord, whose confidence is in Him," I seek to grow a resilient and enduring faith. Like a tree planted by the water, let my faith be nourished by Your word and sustained by Your presence. May I bear the fruits of trust, patience, and steadfastness in all seasons of life.

Help me to withstand the challenges and trials that I may face, using them as opportunities to strengthen my trust in You. Guide me in understanding and applying

Your teachings, so that my faith may be deeply rooted and unwavering.

May my growing faith be a source of inspiration and encouragement to those around me. Let it be a reflection of Your love and faithfulness, drawing others closer to the comfort and hope found in You.

In Jesus' name, I pray, Amen.

Prayer 3: Faith's Journey (Hebrews 11:1)

Merciful Savior, in line with Hebrews 11:1, "Now faith is confidence in what we hope for and assurance about what we do not see," I embark on a journey of growing faith. Help me to see beyond the present circumstances, trusting in Your eternal promises. Strengthen my belief in the unseen, knowing that with You, all things are possible.

In moments of doubt or fear, provide me with the courage to remain steadfast in my faith. Let each challenge be a stepping stone to a deeper trust and understanding of Your will. Help me to embrace each lesson learned along this path, growing closer to You with each step.

May my life be an example of unwavering faith and relentless pursuit of Your truth. Let my growing faith be a testament to Your goodness and a beacon of hope to others seeking to deepen their relationship with You.

In Jesus' name, I pray, Amen.

Prayer 4: Cultivating Steadfast Faith (James 1:3-4)

Heavenly Father, inspired by James 1:3-4, "The testing of your faith produces perseverance," I seek Your guidance in cultivating a steadfast and enduring faith. In times of trial and uncertainty, help me to cling to Your promises and to find strength in Your unwavering love. Teach me the value of perseverance, that through every challenge, my faith may grow stronger and more resilient.

Grant me patience and wisdom to understand the lessons You are teaching me. May each experience, whether joyful or difficult, serve to deepen my trust in You. Let my heart be filled with unshakeable faith, radiating Your love and trustworthiness to those around me.

In Jesus' name, I pray, Amen.

Prayer 5: Nourishing My Faith (Luke 17:5)

Lord, as the apostles asked in Luke 17:5, "Increase our faith," I too seek the nourishment of my faith in Your presence. Encourage me to engage deeply with Your word and to spend time in heartfelt prayer, fostering a closer relationship with You. Help me to see Your hand in every aspect of my life, strengthening my belief and reliance on You.

In moments where my faith feels weak or challenged, remind me of Your constant presence and unwavering support. Let the testimony of Your faithfulness in my life and the lives of others be the soil in which my faith grows and flourishes. May my journey of faith inspire others, showing the transformative power of a life rooted in You.

In Jesus' name, I pray, Amen.

Prayer 6: Walking in Faith (2 Corinthians 5:7)

Merciful Savior, following the message of 2 Corinthians 5:7, "For we live by faith, not by sight," I ask for Your help in walking a path of faith. In a world that often values sight over belief, help me to trust in the unseen - Your grace, Your promises, and Your eternal love. Strengthen my resolve to follow You, even when the road is unclear or the destination unknown.

Guide me through life's uncertainties with faith as my compass. In moments of doubt or fear, anchor me in Your truth, and renew my spirit with hope. May my walk of faith be a journey of continual growth and deepening love for You, a testament to the power of living by faith.

In Jesus' name, I pray,

Amen.

Personal notes:

_____

_____

_____

_____

_____

_____

_____

_____

_____

_____

_____

_____

_____

_____

_____

_____

Prayers before the Bed

Praying before bed is important because it helps you reflect on the day, express gratitude, and seek God's peace and protection for the night. In **Psalm 4:8**, the Bible says, "***In peace I will lie down and sleep, for you alone, Lord, make me dwell in safety***." This verse underscores the security and tranquility that come from entrusting your cares to God before resting. By praying before bed, you can release any worries, ask for forgiveness, and seek guidance for the days ahead, fostering a sense of calm and a restful night's sleep.

Prayer 1: In Peace I Will Lie Down (Psalm 4:8)

Heavenly Father, as Psalm 4:8 reminds us, "In peace I will lie down and sleep, for you alone, Lord, make me dwell in safety," I come to You at the close of this day. Thank You for Your protection and the blessings of this day. As I rest tonight, I ask for Your peace to surround me and for Your presence to be my comfort. Calm my mind from the day's worries and give me restorative sleep.

Guard my heart and mind as I sleep. Let me wake up refreshed and renewed, ready to face the new day with faith and courage. May my dreams be filled with Your wisdom and guidance, and my soul find rest in Your unending love.

In Jesus' name, I pray

Amen.

Prayer 2: The Lord is My Keeper (Psalm 121:5)

Lord, as declared in Psalm 121:5, "The Lord is your keeper; the Lord is your shade on your right hand," I seek Your protection and comfort this night. As I end this day, I entrust myself and my loved ones into Your caring hands. Provide a safe haven for us, shielding us from harm and guiding us through the night.

Help me to release all my concerns and burdens to You, trusting in Your wisdom and timing. Let Your peace fill my heart, knowing that You are always with me. May my sleep be peaceful and restful, under the watchful care of Your loving presence.

In Jesus' name, I pray, Amen.

Prayer 3: Under His Wings (Psalm 91:4)

Merciful Savior, inspired by Psalm 91:4, "He will cover you with his feathers, and under his wings you will find refuge," I seek Your protection and comfort as night falls. Wrap me in Your peace as I lay down to rest. Help me to let go of the day's challenges and to find solace in Your loving care.

Watch over me and my loved ones throughout the night. Let Your angels guard us, and Your Spirit soothe our minds. May we awake in the morning renewed and strengthened, filled with Your joy and ready to embrace the blessings of a new day.

In Jesus' name, I pray, Amen.

Prayer 4: Guard Us Through the Night (Psalm 4:8)

Heavenly Father, as Psalm 4:8 reassures, "In peace I will lie down and sleep, for you alone, Lord, make me dwell in safety," I come to You at the close of this day. Thank You for Your guidance and care. As I lay down to rest, I ask for Your protection through the night. Calm my mind from the day's worries, and let Your peace envelop me, ensuring a restful and rejuvenating sleep.

Watch over me and my loved ones, Lord. Keep us safe from harm and shield us from all evil. Let Your angels guard us and Your love comfort us. As we rest in Your embrace, renew our spirits, preparing us for the challenges and blessings of tomorrow.

In Jesus' name, I pray, Amen.

Prayer 5: Rest in Your Faithfulness (Lamentations 3:22-23)

Lord, in the comforting words of Lamentations 3:22-23, "The steadfast love of the Lord never ceases; his mercies never come to an end; they are new every morning," I find solace. As night descends, I thank You for the steadfast love and unending mercies You have shown throughout this day. Help me to rest in the assurance of Your faithfulness, releasing all my concerns into Your capable hands.

Quiet my heart and mind, O Lord, and grant me a peaceful night's sleep. Renew my strength and fill my heart with hope for the new day. May I awake with gratitude, ready to embrace Your new mercies and to walk in the path You have set before me.

In Jesus' name, I pray, Amen.

Prayer 6: Under Your Watchful Eye (Psalm 121:3-4)

Merciful Savior, as Psalm 121:3-4 promises, "He will not let your foot slip—he who watches over you will not slumber," I entrust myself to Your care this night. Thank You for watching over me today, and I ask that You continue to keep me safe as I sleep. May Your presence provide comfort and assurance, warding off fears and anxieties.

Let Your peace reign in my heart tonight. Protect me from the distractions and disturbances of the night, and grant me a restful sleep. I look forward to the dawn, knowing that Your love and protection are constant, and Your mercies are renewed with each morning.

In Jesus' name, I pray, Amen.

Prayer 7: Evening Rest in Your Care (Psalm 4:8)

Heavenly Father, as we find solace in the words of Psalm 4:8, "In peace I will lie down and sleep, for you alone, Lord, make me dwell in safety," I come to You this evening. I thank You for the blessings and lessons of this day. As the night falls, I seek Your peace and comfort, trusting in Your loving care to provide rest and rejuvenation for my body and soul.

In the quiet of this night, I lay down all my worries and burdens at Your feet. Grant me a restful sleep free of anxieties, knowing that You are always watching over me. Let Your presence be the calming force in my life, soothing my thoughts and easing my heart.

As I close my eyes tonight, I entrust myself and my loved ones into Your protective embrace. Watch over us through the night, and lead us into a new day filled with Your grace and mercy. May we wake refreshed and ready to embrace the opportunities and challenges ahead.

In Jesus' name, I pray, Amen.

Prayer 8: Guardian of My Soul (Psalm 121:5-6)

Lord, as expressed in Psalm 121:5-6, "The Lord is your keeper; the Lord is your shade on your right hand," I come before You at the end of this day. Your watchful care has been my shield and comfort. As darkness falls, I ask for Your continued protection over me and my family. May Your presence be a reassuring guard through the hours of this night.

I seek solace in Your promises, releasing the stresses and strains of the day into Your capable hands. Guide my thoughts towards peace and my heart towards tranquility. In the silence of this night, fill my mind with reflections of Your love, grace, and the many blessings You bestow upon us.

As I prepare for sleep, surround me with Your peace. Let Your angels watch over my home, bringing a sense of security and calm. May I awake with a renewed spirit, ready to walk in Your light and to embrace Your plans for me.

In Jesus' name, I pray, Amen.

Prayer 9: Beneath Your Stars (Genesis 1:16)

Merciful Savior, under the vastness of Your sky, as Genesis 1:16 illuminates, "God made two great lights–the greater light to govern the day and the lesser light to govern the night," I pause to reflect on Your majesty and creativity. The night sky, a canvas of Your design, reminds me of Your infinite power and wisdom. As I settle into the quiet of this evening, I am filled with awe and gratitude for the wonders of Your creation.

In this moment of nighttime stillness, I seek Your comfort and reassurance. Calm any turmoil within me and grant me a peaceful mind. Help me to surrender the events of today, both the joys and the challenges, into Your loving hands, trusting that You work all things for good.

As I rest under Your stars, let me be reminded of Your presence in every aspect of my life. Grant me restful sleep, secure in the knowledge that You are my guardian and guide. May tomorrow bring a fresh start, new opportunities to serve You, and continued awareness of Your constant love.

In Jesus' name, I pray, Amen.

Prayer 10: Evening Reflections (Psalm 4:8)

Heavenly Father, as Psalm 4:8 reminds us, "In peace I will both lie down and sleep; for you alone, O Lord, make me dwell in safety," I come to You in gratitude for the day that has passed. I reflect on the moments of joy and challenge, and I thank You for Your presence in each of them. As night envelops the world, I seek Your peace and protection, trusting in Your loving care to guide me through the hours of darkness.

In the quiet of this night, I lay before You my worries and burdens, seeking Your comfort and reassurance. Help me to release my anxieties and rest in the knowledge that You are always with me. Let Your peace fill my heart, calming my thoughts and preparing me for restful sleep.

As I close my eyes tonight, I pray for Your watchful eye to remain upon me and my loved ones. Guard us through the night, and lead us into a new day filled with Your mercy and grace. May we awaken refreshed and ready to follow Your path, carrying the peace and love You have granted us.

In Jesus' name, I pray, Amen.

Prayer 11: Nighttime Sanctuary (Psalm 91:1-2)

Lord, in the comfort of Psalm 91:1-2, "He who dwells in the shelter of the Most High will abide in the shadow of the Almighty," I find solace as I prepare for rest. I acknowledge Your sovereignty over my life and the world around me. As I settle into the night, I seek refuge in Your presence, knowing that You are my fortress and my sanctuary against the uncertainties of life.

I pray for Your healing touch on my body and mind, soothing the weariness of the day. May Your loving arms envelop me, granting peace and tranquility as I sleep. Help me to let go of any fears or concerns, resting securely in the knowledge that You are in control.

Awaken in me a renewed sense of purpose and hope as I face a new day. Strengthen my faith and resolve to serve You faithfully. Let each morning remind me of Your unfailing love and the endless opportunities to witness Your grace in my life.

In Jesus' name, I pray, Amen.

Prayer 12: Under the Stars of Grace (Genesis 1:16)

Merciful Savior, as Genesis 1:16 speaks of the greater and lesser lights to govern the day and night, I am reminded of Your magnificent creation. The stars above are a testament to Your glory and power. As I gaze upon the night sky, I am filled with awe and gratitude for the vastness of Your love and the beauty of the world You have created. I thank You for this day, for its challenges and its blessings, and for Your guiding hand through it all.

In the stillness of this night, I seek Your grace and forgiveness for any shortcomings. Help me to learn from the experiences of this day and to grow in wisdom and love. May my heart find rest in Your promises, and may my spirit be rejuvenated by Your peace.

As I lay down to sleep, I ask for Your protection over me and those I hold dear. Let Your angels watch over us, and may Your presence be our comfort and shield. I look forward to the dawn, ready to embrace the new day with a heart full of Your love and a spirit eager to serve You.

In Jesus' name, I pray

Amen.

Personal notes:

_____

_____

_____

_____

_____

_____

_____

_____

_____

_____

_____

_____

_____

Sunrise Prayers

Sunrise prayers are important because they allow you to start your day with a sense of purpose and alignment with God's will. In **Psalm 5:3**, the Bible says, "*In the morning, Lord, you hear my voice; in the morning I lay my requests before you and wait expectantly.*" This verse highlights the significance of beginning your day in communication with God, seeking His guidance and blessing. By dedicating the first moments of the day to prayer, you set a positive and focused tone for the day ahead, drawing strength and inspiration from your connection with God.

Prayer 1: New Mercies at Dawn (Lamentations 3:22-23)

Heavenly Father, as Lamentations 3:22-23 declares, "The steadfast love of the Lord never ceases; his mercies never come to an end; they are new every morning," I greet this new day with a heart full of gratitude. Thank You for the gift of this fresh morning, symbolizing the new opportunities and blessings that lie ahead. As the first light of dawn breaks the horizon, I am reminded of

Your faithfulness and the renewal that comes with each sunrise.

Today, guide my steps and my decisions. Help me to embrace each moment with a spirit of thankfulness and to reflect Your love in all my interactions. May this day be filled with the evidence of Your presence in my life, and may I be an instrument of Your peace and kindness in the world around me.

In Jesus' name, I pray

Amen.

Prayer 2: Awaken to Your Light (Psalm 5:3)

Lord, in the spirit of Psalm 5:3, "In the morning, Lord, you hear my voice; in the morning I lay my requests before you and wait expectantly," I come before You at the start of this day. I offer You my hopes, dreams, and plans, and I seek Your wisdom and guidance. As the sun rises, bringing light to the world, let Your light illuminate my heart and mind, guiding me in the path of righteousness.

Bless this day with Your presence, O Lord. May my words and actions be pleasing to You. Help me to be attentive to Your voice and responsive to Your leading. May this day be a testimony to the joy and peace that come from walking in Your light.

In Jesus' name, I pray,

Amen.

Prayer 3: Morning Praise and Purpose (Psalm 59:16)

Merciful Savior, as Psalm 59:16 reminds us, "But I will sing of your strength, in the morning I will sing of your love; for you are my fortress, my refuge in times of trouble," I begin this day with praise for Your unending strength and love. As the morning sun heralds the start of a new day, let my heart be filled with joy and gratitude for Your constant protection and guidance.

As I embark on the tasks of this day, grant me the courage to face challenges with faith and the wisdom to make choices that honor You. Let my life be a reflection of Your grace, spreading hope and light to everyone I encounter. May this day not only be about accomplishing tasks but also about growing closer to You and fulfilling the purpose You have set for me.

In Jesus' name, I pray, Amen.

Prayer 4: Embrace the New Day (Psalm 118:24)

Heavenly Father, as Psalm 118:24 proclaims, "This is the day that the Lord has made; let us rejoice and be glad in it," I welcome the arrival of this new day. With the rising sun, I am reminded of Your faithfulness and the fresh start that each day brings. I thank You for the rest of the night and the promise of today. As the first rays of sunlight touch the earth, I ask for Your guidance and strength to face whatever this day holds.

Fill my heart with joy and gratitude for the gift of life. Help me to see the beauty in every moment and to seize the opportunities You provide. Let this day be one where I draw closer to You, reflecting Your love and grace in all that I do.

In Jesus' name, I pray,

Amen.

Prayer 5: Morning Renewal (Lamentations 3:22-23)

Lord, echoing the words of Lamentations 3:22-23, "The steadfast love of the Lord never ceases; his mercies never come to an end; they are new every morning," I stand in awe of Your unending love as a new day dawns. Thank You for Your mercies that are renewed each morning. As the sun rises, it brings hope and a reminder of Your constant presence in my life.

I pray for the wisdom to recognize Your hand in all things and the courage to embrace the challenges and joys of this day. May I walk in Your love, spreading kindness and peace wherever I go. Let this day be a testament to Your goodness and a reflection of the hope that I find in You.

In Jesus' name, I pray

Amen.

Prayer 6: Dawn of Hope (Psalm 5:3)

Merciful Savior, as Psalm 5:3 says, "In the morning, Lord, you hear my voice; in the morning I lay my requests before you and wait expectantly," I greet this day with hope and expectation. As the sky brightens with the morning light, I lay before You my hopes, fears, and dreams. Thank You for the promise of a new day, a canvas to paint with acts of love, kindness, and faith.

As I step into this day, guide my actions and words. Help me to be a source of encouragement and light to those I encounter. May my life today be a living prayer, a testament to Your grace and an expression of my faith in You.

In Jesus' name, I pray, Amen.

Prayer 7: Dawn of a New Beginning (Psalm 5:3)

Heavenly Father, as the psalmist declares in Psalm 5:3, "In the morning, Lord, you hear my voice; in the morning I lay my requests before you and wait expectantly," I come to You at the break of dawn. With the first light piercing through the darkness, I am reminded of Your constant renewal and the hope that each new day brings. I thank You for the rest of the night and for the gift of this fresh morning, a symbol of Your unfailing love and new opportunities.

As the world awakens, I seek Your wisdom and guidance for the day ahead. Help me to align my thoughts, words, and actions with Your will. May this day be filled with moments that glorify You, as I navigate through both challenges and joys, keeping my eyes firmly fixed on You.

Bless this day, Lord, and use it for Your purpose. Guide me in making a positive impact on those I encounter and in spreading Your love and kindness. Let the light of this new day reflect in my life, illuminating the path You have set before me and shining Your grace into the lives of others.

In Jesus' name, I pray

Amen.

Prayer 8: Morning's Promise of Grace (Lamentations 3:22-23)

Lord, in the spirit of Lamentations 3:22-23, "The steadfast love of the Lord never ceases; his mercies never come to an end; they are new every morning," I greet this day with a heart full of gratitude. Thank You for the promise of Your never-ending mercy and love that each sunrise brings. As I witness the beauty of this morning, I am filled with a renewed sense of Your presence and grace in my life.

I pray for Your guiding hand over all my endeavors today. Help me to embrace each opportunity and challenge with faith and courage, trusting in Your providential care. May this day be a journey of discovering more of Your love and sharing it with those around me.

Renew my spirit, O God, as the sun renews the earth. Let me walk in Your light, radiating hope and peace to everyone I meet. May this day be a testimony to Your goodness and a reflection of the joy and peace found in walking with You.

In Jesus' name, I pray,

Amen.

Prayer 9: Embracing the Light of a New Day (Psalm 118:24)

Merciful Savior, as we are reminded in Psalm 118:24, "This is the day the Lord has made; let us rejoice and be glad in it," I embrace the fresh start that this morning offers. As the sun rises, bringing light and warmth to the world, I acknowledge Your creative power and thank You for the blessings of life. This new day is a precious gift from You, filled with potential and hope.

Guide me today in Your wisdom and truth. Help me to live out this day fully, making the most of every opportunity to serve and honor You. Let my words and actions reflect Your love and grace, as I seek to be a light in the places You have placed me.

As the day unfolds, I trust in Your guidance and provision. May my heart be open to Your teachings, and my hands ready to do Your work. Let this day be one of growth, service, and love, all for Your glory and honor.

In Jesus' name, I pray

Amen.

Prayer 10: Awakening to God's Glory (Psalm 19:1-2)

Heavenly Father, as Psalm 19:1-2 declares, "The heavens declare the glory of God; the skies proclaim the work of his hands," I stand in awe of Your creation at this sunrise. The beauty of the dawn, with its vibrant colors and gentle light, reminds me of Your majesty and the perfection of Your designs. I thank You for this new day, a fresh canvas to paint with acts of kindness, moments of reflection, and opportunities to glorify Your name.

As the world wakes up, I pray for the wisdom to navigate this day in a way that honors You. Help me to recognize Your presence in every moment, to listen for Your guidance, and to act with compassion and integrity.

May this day be a journey of discovery, where I not only learn more about You but also about the depth of Your love for me and all of creation.

Bless this day, Lord, and make it fruitful. Guide my thoughts, words, and deeds to align with Your will. Let me be a light to those around me, a beacon of Your love and hope, and may everything I do today bring glory to Your name.

In Jesus' name, I pray, Amen.

Prayer 11: Morning's Fresh Mercy (Lamentations 3:22-23)

Lord, inspired by Lamentations 3:22-23, "The steadfast love of the Lord never ceases; his mercies never come to an end; they are new every morning," I greet this day with a grateful heart. Your mercies are as fresh as the morning dew, and Your love is as radiant as the sunrise. As this new day begins, I am reminded of the countless ways You have shown Your faithfulness to me.

I ask for Your guidance as I step into the challenges and joys of this day. Help me to walk in Your path, to spread kindness and joy wherever I go, and to face each situation with the courage and wisdom that comes from You. May I be attuned to the needs of others, serving them with the love and compassion that You have shown to me.

As the sun rises, let it bring not only light to my world but also enlightenment to my soul. Strengthen my faith and deepen my understanding of Your ways. May this day be an opportunity to grow closer to You and to reflect Your love in all my interactions.

In Jesus' name, I pray, Amen.

Prayer 12: Embrace the Light of Today (Psalm 118:24)

Merciful Savior, reflecting on Psalm 118:24, "This is the day the Lord has made; we will rejoice and be glad in it," I welcome the light of this new day with open arms. The sunrise marks the beginning of new possibilities, a reminder of Your endless creativity and the gift of life. As the day unfolds, I cherish the opportunity to experience Your grace, to learn, to grow, and to make a difference in the world.

I pray for the strength and courage to face the day's tasks and trials. Help me to embrace each moment with joy, to tackle challenges with faith, and to find peace in knowing that You are with me every step of the way. May

I use the time given to me today to be a testament to Your love, showing patience, kindness, and understanding to those I meet.

Let this day be filled with moments of praise and worship, celebrating Your glory and goodness. Guide me in my decisions, protect me in my journey, and let my actions reflect the beauty of Your creation. May this day be a beautiful expression of the life and love You have so generously bestowed upon me.

In Jesus' name, I pray, Amen.

Personal notes:

_____

_____

_____

_____

_____

_____

_____

_____

Morning Prayers

Thanking God when you wake up is important because it sets a positive and grateful tone for your entire day. In **Lamentations 3:22-23**, the Bible says, "***Because of the Lord's great love we are not consumed, for his compassions never fail. They are new every morning; great is your faithfulness***." This verse reminds you of God's constant love and faithfulness, renewed each day. By expressing gratitude to God upon waking, you acknowledge His blessings, embrace a mindset of thankfulness, and invite His presence into your daily activities.

Prayer 1: Morning Gratitude (Psalm 5:3)

Heavenly Father, as Psalm 5:3 says, "In the morning, Lord, you hear my voice; in the morning I lay my requests before you and wait expectantly," I come to You with a heart full of gratitude for this new day. Thank You for the restful night and the gift of awakening to new possibilities and opportunities to serve You. As the day begins, I place all my plans and hopes in Your hands, trusting in Your perfect will.

Guide me through this day in wisdom and understanding. Help me to see Your hand in every situation, to respond with love and kindness, and to be a reflection of Your grace to those around me. May I make the most of this day, using each moment to glorify You and to spread Your love.

In Jesus' name, I pray, Amen.

Prayer 2: Seeking Guidance at Daybreak (Psalm 143:8)

Lord, inspired by Psalm 143:8, "Let the morning bring me word of your unfailing love," I seek Your presence at the start of this day. As the sun rises, so does my spirit, uplifted by the hope and renewal that each new day brings. I ask for Your guidance and clarity, that I may walk in Your path and align my actions with Your purposes.

Fill me with Your wisdom and strength to face the day's challenges. Let me be a beacon of Your peace and compassion in a world that often feels chaotic and uncertain. May my words and deeds be a testimony of Your love and an encouragement to those I encounter.

In Jesus' name, I pray, Amen.

Prayer 3: Embracing the Day's Blessings (Psalm 118:24)

Merciful Savior, reflecting on Psalm 118:24, "This is the day the Lord has made; let us rejoice and be glad in it," I embrace this morning with joy and anticipation. I am grateful for Your constant presence in my life and the fresh opportunities this day presents. Help me to recognize the blessings in every moment and to be an instrument of Your grace and goodness.

As I go about my day, let Your love guide my actions and Your wisdom influence my decisions. May I find joy in serving others and peace in knowing that I am walking in Your light. Let this day be a celebration of the life You have given me, filled with purpose, love, and joy.

In Jesus' name, I pray, Amen.

Prayer 4: Joy Comes in the Morning (Psalm 30:5)

Heavenly Father, as Psalm 30:5 reminds us, "Weeping may stay for the night, but rejoicing comes in the morning," I welcome this new day with a heart open to Your blessings and lessons. Thank You for the gift of life and the fresh opportunities that this morning brings. As the sun rises, filling the sky with its warm hues, I am filled with gratitude for Your constant love and renewed hope.

Guide me today in Your wisdom and truth. Help me to face each challenge with courage and to embrace each joy with gratitude. Let my words and actions reflect Your love and bring comfort and encouragement to those around me. May this day be a testament to Your grace and a reflection of the hope that dwells within me through Your love.

In Jesus' name, I pray

Amen.

Prayer 5: Seeking God's Guidance (Proverbs 3:6)

Lord, in the spirit of Proverbs 3:6, "In all your ways submit to him, and he will make your paths straight," I start this day seeking Your guidance and presence in every aspect of my life. As the world awakens, let my heart and mind also awaken to Your will and purpose. Thank You for the promise of Your guidance and the assurance that when I trust in You, my path will be clear.

Grant me the discernment to make wise decisions and the strength to follow through with my commitments.

Help me to show Your love and grace in my interactions and to be a light to those I encounter. May this day be filled with acts of kindness, moments of reflection, and opportunities to glorify Your name.

In Jesus' name, I pray, Amen.

Prayer 6: Embracing Each Moment (Ecclesiastes 3:1)

Merciful Savior, as Ecclesiastes 3:1 declares, "There is a time for everything, and a season for every activity under the heavens," I welcome this day as a precious gift from You. With each passing moment, help me to embrace the time You have given me, to use it wisely, and to appreciate the unique blessings of today. Thank You for the rhythm of life, the change of seasons, and the promise that You are with me in every moment.

As I go about my day, let me be mindful of the needs of others, quick to listen, slow to speak, and eager to offer help. Let me find joy in simple pleasures and be content in the knowledge that You are in control. May my actions today bring honor to Your name and spread Your love and peace to all I meet.

In Jesus' name, I pray, Amen.

Prayer 7: Awaken to His Mercies (Lamentations 3:22-23)

Heavenly Father, as declared in Lamentations 3:22-23, "The steadfast love of the Lord never ceases; His mercies never come to an end; they are new every morning," I rise today embracing the freshness of Your mercy and love. With the dawn of this new day, I am reminded of Your endless grace and the opportunities that lie ahead. Thank You for the gift of life, for the breath that sustains me, and for the chance to experience Your love anew.

I pray for the wisdom to navigate this day according to Your will. May Your Spirit guide my decisions, strengthen my heart, and illuminate my path. Help me to see Your hand in every detail of my life, recognizing the blessings You pour out continuously. Let me be a vessel of Your peace, showing kindness and compassion to all I encounter.

As the sun rises, casting away the shadows, let Your light shine through me, dispelling darkness wherever I go. May my words speak life and my actions reflect Your love. I entrust this day to You, confident in Your care and guidance. May I live fully in each moment, grateful for Your presence and steadfast in my faith.

In Jesus' name, I pray, Amen.

Prayer 8: Guided by Your Light (Psalm 119:105)

Lord, Psalm 119:105 tells us, "Your word is a lamp for my feet, a light on my path." As I greet the morning, I seek Your illumination in every step I take. Your Word is the foundation upon which I build my day, offering direction, comfort, and wisdom. Thank You for the promises that light up my way, ensuring I never walk in darkness when I follow You.

Today, I ask for discernment and clarity in my thoughts and actions. Let me be attuned to Your voice, responsive to Your leading, and sensitive to Your prompting. In a world filled with noise and distractions, help me to focus on what truly matters, dedicating my efforts to tasks that bring honor to Your name and blessing to others.

May this day be marked by Your presence in my life, shaping me to be more like You. Let my heart be open to learning new lessons of faith, courage, and love. I commit my plans to You, trusting that You will align them with Your perfect will. May my life today be a testament to the transformative power of Your Word and love.

In Jesus' name, I pray

Amen.

Prayer 9: Embrace the Day with Praise (Psalm 118:24)

Merciful Savior, echoing Psalm 118:24, "This is the day that the Lord has made; let us rejoice and be glad in it," I welcome this morning with a song of praise in my heart. Each sunrise is a reminder of Your faithfulness and a call to celebrate the life You have bestowed upon us. I am grateful for Your enduring love, which renews us and offers hope and strength for the journey ahead.

I pray for a heart filled with gratitude and eyes that see the beauty in Your creation. May I approach this day with a spirit of thankfulness, recognizing even the smallest of blessings as gifts from Your hand. Help me to spread joy and encouragement, lifting the spirits of those around me and pointing them to the source of all goodness.

Guide me in my endeavors today, that I may act justly, love mercy, and walk humbly with You. Strengthen me to face the challenges of the day with grace and resilience, always mindful of Your sovereignty and love. Let my life be a reflection of Your glory, serving as a beacon of hope and love in a world in need.

In Jesus' name, I pray

Amen.

Personal notes:

_____

_____

_____

_____

_____

_____

_____

_____

_____

_____

_____

_____

_____

_____

_____

_____

Meditation Prayers

Meditation is a valuable practice that helps you to center your mind, reflect on God's word, and cultivate a deeper relationship with Him. In **Joshua 1:8**, the Bible says, "***Keep this Book of the Law always on your lips; meditate on it day and night, so that you may be careful to do everything written in it. Then you will be prosperous and successful.***" This verse emphasizes the importance of meditating on scripture to align your thoughts and actions with God's will. By incorporating meditation into your daily routine, you can find peace, clarity, and spiritual growth.

Prayer 1: In Stillness and Trust (Isaiah 30:15)

Heavenly Father, as Isaiah 30:15 reminds us, "In quietness and in trust shall be your strength," I come before You seeking tranquility in the midst of life's storms. In this moment of meditation, I quiet my mind and focus on Your unchanging nature. Help me to find strength in stillness, to listen for Your gentle whispers amidst the chaos of the world. Your presence brings peace that surpasses all understanding, and in this sacred space, I seek to draw nearer to You.

Teach me, Lord, to trust in Your timing and Your perfect plan. As I meditate on Your word and Your goodness, fill my heart with the assurance that You are in control. Let this time of quiet reflection renew my spirit, giving me a deeper understanding of Your love and a greater appreciation for the many ways You work in my life.

In these moments of contemplation, I lay down my worries and fears at Your feet. Grant me the wisdom to discern Your will and the courage to follow where You lead. May this time of meditation be a foundation upon which my faith is strengthened and my soul is refreshed. Let me emerge from this time more aligned with Your will, ready to face the challenges and joys that await.

In Jesus' name, I pray, Amen.

Prayer 2: Seeking the Shepherd's Guidance (Psalm 23:1-3)

Lord, in the words of Psalm 23, "The Lord is my shepherd; I shall not want. He makes me lie down in green pastures. He leads me beside still waters. He restores my soul," I find comfort and guidance. In this time of meditation, I seek to deepen my relationship with You, my Shepherd. Guide me to the green pastures of Your truth and the still waters of Your peace. In the hustle of life, remind me of the importance of resting in Your presence and drawing from the well of Your wisdom.

As I meditate on Your word, open my heart to receive Your teachings. Help me to understand the depth of Your love and to trust in Your provision. May this time be a journey of spiritual growth, where I learn to rely more fully on Your guidance and less on my own understanding.

Let me find restoration for my soul as I reflect on Your faithfulness and goodness. Strengthen me to walk the paths of righteousness, keeping my eyes fixed on You, the author and perfecter of my faith. May this meditation be a time of sweet communion with You, where I am reminded of Your constant care and unfailing love.

In Jesus' name, I pray

Amen.

Prayer 3: Rooted in Love (Ephesians 3:17-18)

Merciful Savior, Ephesians 3:17-18 encourages us, "That Christ may dwell in your hearts through faith. That you, being rooted and grounded in love, may have strength to comprehend with all the saints what is the breadth and length and height and depth." As I enter this time of meditation, I focus on being rooted and grounded in Your love. Help me to comprehend the vastness of Your love, which surpasses all knowledge and fills me with the fullness of God.

In these moments of quiet reflection, let my heart be open to the transformative power of Your love. May it permeate every aspect of my being, bringing healing, wholeness, and a deeper sense of Your presence in my life. Teach me to love as You love, extending grace and compassion to those around me.

Strengthen me, Lord, to live a life that reflects Your love to the world. May my actions be a testament to the depth of Your love and my words be an encouragement to others. In this meditation, let me be reminded of the privilege of being a vessel of Your love, called to share it freely and unconditionally.

In Jesus' name, I pray, Amen.

Prayer 4: Seeking Serenity in His Presence (Psalm 46:10)

Heavenly Father, as Psalm 46:10 says, "Be still, and know that I am God," I come before You in meditation, seeking serenity in Your divine presence. In the quiet moments of this morning, I pause to acknowledge Your sovereignty over my life and the world. Help me to let go of my anxieties and concerns, to find peace in the knowledge that You are in control. Your presence is a sanctuary, a place where my soul finds rest and my spirit is rejuvenated.

In this time of stillness, I ask for clarity and guidance. May Your Holy Spirit speak into my life, bringing wisdom and insight. Let this meditative practice deepen my understanding of Your will, making me more receptive to Your gentle nudges and guiding whispers. I long to align my desires with Yours, to be molded by Your hands, and to grow in grace and truth.

As I sit in contemplation, fill me with a sense of Your love and purpose. Strengthen me for the day ahead, infusing my actions with kindness and my words with love. May this time of meditation be a foundation for a day lived in harmony with Your will, a day where every moment is an opportunity to glorify You and serve others in Your name.

In Jesus' name, I pray,

Amen.

Prayer 5: Rooted in His Love (Ephesians 3:17-18)

Lord, inspired by Ephesians 3:17-18, "So that Christ may dwell in your hearts through faith—that you, being rooted and grounded in love, may have strength to comprehend with all the saints what is the breadth and length and height and depth," I enter this time of meditation with a desire to be rooted and grounded in Your love. I seek to understand the vastness of Your love, a love that surpasses all knowledge and fills me with the fullness of God. In these quiet moments, let my heart be open to the transformative power of Your love.

I pray for a deeper connection with You, my Creator and Sustainer. May this meditative practice be a channel through which I experience Your presence more fully. Help me to let go of worldly distractions, to focus my thoughts on Your goodness, and to cultivate a heart that is responsive to Your calling. I yearn for a deeper faith, one that is nourished by Your word and strengthened by Your Spirit.

As I meditate on Your love, let it permeate every aspect of my being. May it guide my actions, shape my interactions, and be the foundation upon which I build my life. Let this meditation remind me of the privilege of being Your child, called to love as You have loved us, freely and unconditionally.

In Jesus' name, I pray, Amen.

Prayer 6: Abiding in His Peace (John 16:33)

Merciful Savior, in John 16:33, You assure us, "In the world you will have tribulation. But take heart; I have overcome the world." In this meditation, I seek to abide in the peace You offer, a peace that transcends all understanding. Help me to embrace the assurance of Your victory over the world, letting go of fear and embracing faith. In the calmness of this moment, I find solace in Your promise of peace and the knowledge that You are with me always.

I ask for the strength to face the challenges of life with a peaceful heart. May this time of quiet reflection anchor me in Your truth, keeping me steady amidst life's storms. Teach me to rely on Your strength, not my own, and to trust in Your perfect plan. Let this meditation be a reminder of Your constant presence and the unwavering peace that comes from trusting in You.

As I continue through my day, let the peace I find in this meditation permeate my thoughts, words, and actions. May it influence how I interact with others, bringing calmness and understanding into every conversation and situation. Help me to be a vessel of Your peace, spreading hope and encouragement to those around me, shining Your light in a world in need.

In Jesus' name, I pray, Amen.

Prayer 7: Embracing God's Peace (Philippians 4:7)

Heavenly Father, inspired by Philippians 4:7, "And the peace of God, which surpasses all understanding, will guard your hearts and your minds in Christ Jesus," I enter this time of meditation. In the stillness, I seek to experience the depth of Your peace, a tranquility that transcends the chaos of the world. As I quiet my mind and focus on Your presence, let Your peace envelop me, protecting my heart and mind from the worries of life.

In this sacred moment of contemplation, I surrender my fears, anxieties, and uncertainties to You. Help me to trust in Your providence and timing, knowing that You are with me every step of the way. May Your peace reign in my heart, guiding my thoughts and actions throughout the day. Let me be a vessel of Your calmness, sharing Your peace with those I encounter.

As I meditate on Your Word and Your promises, strengthen my faith and deepen my understanding of Your love. Let this time of meditation be a refuge where I am reminded of Your constant care and where my spirit is renewed. May I carry this peace with me as I go about my day, confident in Your presence and steadfast in my trust in You.

In Jesus' name, I pray, Amen.

Prayer 8: In the Shadow of His Wings (Psalm 91:1)

Lord, echoing Psalm 91:1, "He who dwells in the shelter of the Most High will abide in the shadow of the Almighty," I come to You in meditation, seeking refuge in

Your presence. As I focus on Your steadfast love and protection, let me feel the security of being under Your wings. In the quiet of this moment, I find solace in Your promise to be my shelter and fortress.

I pray for the awareness of Your constant presence in my life. Help me to recognize Your guiding hand in every circumstance and to feel the comfort of Your protective embrace. In this time of meditation, let me draw closer to You, finding strength and courage in Your proximity. Remind me that no matter what challenges I face, I am never alone; You are always there, offering Your love and support.

As I sit in contemplation of Your love and faithfulness, fill my heart with gratitude and my mind with peace. May this meditation strengthen my relationship with You, building a foundation of trust and reliance on Your unwavering protection. Let me emerge from this time reassured of Your care, ready to face the world with confidence and peace, knowing You are always by my side.

In Jesus' name, I pray

Amen.

Prayer 9: Rooted in His Love (Ephesians 3:17)

Merciful Savior, as stated in Ephesians 3:17, "So that Christ may dwell in your hearts through faith–that you, being rooted and grounded in love," I enter this meditation focused on being deeply rooted in Your love. Let this time be an opportunity to deepen my understanding of the vastness of Your love, a love that encompasses, heals, and empowers. May I become more aware of the presence of Christ within me, growing in faith and rooted in the assurance of Your love.

I ask for Your guidance to live a life anchored in Your love, reflecting Your compassion and grace in my interactions with others. Help me to embody the qualities of Your love: patience, kindness, and humility. In this meditative practice, let me explore the dimensions of Your love, understanding its breadth, length, height, and depth, and being transformed by it.

May this meditation enrich my spiritual journey, drawing me closer to You and strengthening my commitment to live according to Your will. Let the knowledge of Your love inspire me to extend grace and kindness to those around me, acting as a testament to the transformative power of Your love in my life.

In Jesus' name, I pray, Amen.

Personal notes:

_____

_____

_____

_____

_____

_____

_____

_____

_____

_____

_____

_____

_____

_____

_____

_____

Protection Prayers

Protection prayers are vital as they invite God's safeguarding presence into your life, offering comfort and security amidst uncertainties and dangers. In **Psalm 91:1-2**, the Bible declares, "***Whoever dwells in the shelter of the Most High will rest in the shadow of the Almighty. I will say of the Lord, 'He is my refuge and my fortress, my God, in whom I trust.'***" This verse emphasizes God's promise of protection for those who seek refuge in Him. By praying for protection, you entrust your safety to God, acknowledging His power and seeking His guidance and defense in all circumstances.

Prayer 1: Under His Wings (Psalm 91:4)

Heavenly Father, inspired by Psalm 91:4, "He will cover you with his feathers, and under his wings you will find refuge; his faithfulness will be your shield and rampart," I seek Your protection against the evils of this world. In the shadow of Your wings, I find safety and comfort, knowing that no harm can withstand Your mighty power. Shield me, Lord, from the snares of the enemy and the temptations that seek to lead me astray.

I ask for Your vigilant watch over my life and the lives of my loved ones. Surround us with Your angels, and let Your presence be a constant guardian. In moments of doubt and fear, remind me of Your unfailing protection and strength. May Your armor be my defense, and Your Word my guiding light in the darkness. Keep me safe in Your loving embrace, and let no evil befall me.

In Jesus' name, I pray,

Amen.

Prayer 2: The Lord is My Fortress (2 Samuel 22:2)

Lord, echoing the words of 2 Samuel 22:2, "The Lord is my rock, my fortress and my deliverer," I come before You seeking refuge from the evils that lurk in the shadows. Be my rock and my fortress, a place of safety where I can stand firm against the challenges and threats of this world. Protect me from harm and guide me on a path of righteousness.

Grant me the discernment to recognize the works of evil and the strength to resist its allure. In Your mighty name, let every plan of the adversary be thwarted and every attack be repelled. I place my trust in You, confident that Your power and love are greater than any force of darkness. Safeguard my heart and mind, and let me dwell in the peace of Your protection.

In Jesus' name, I pray,

Amen.

Prayer 3: A Shield About Me (Psalm 3:3)

Merciful Savior, as declared in Psalm 3:3, "But you, Lord, are a shield around me, my glory, the One who lifts my head high," I seek Your divine protection in a world filled with uncertainty and malevolence. Be a shield around me and my loved ones, guarding us from the influences of evil. Lift us above the fears and dangers that surround us, keeping us safe in Your providential care.

In the face of adversity and wickedness, let Your strength be my comfort and Your wisdom my guide. Protect my mind from deceitful thoughts and my heart from corruption. May Your Holy Spirit dwell within me, guiding my actions and strengthening my resolve to walk in Your ways. Let me rest in the assurance of Your encompassing protection, trusting in Your power to overcome all evil.

In Jesus' name, I pray, Amen.

Prayer 4: Deliver Us from Evil (Matthew 6:13)

Heavenly Father, in the spirit of Matthew 6:13, "And lead us not into temptation, but deliver us from evil," I come before You seeking Your protection and guidance. As I navigate through the challenges and uncertainties of life, shield me from the snares of evil and temptation. Your wisdom and strength are my refuge; in You, I find the courage to stand firm against the forces that seek to harm me or lead me astray.

I ask for Your watchful eye to be upon me and those I hold dear. Guard our hearts and minds from the deceptions and malice of the enemy. In moments of weakness, be our fortress and our deliverer. May Your presence be a constant reminder of the victory we have in You, keeping us safe from all harm and leading us on the path of righteousness for Your name's sake.

In Jesus' name, I pray

Amen.

Prayer 5: Our Refuge and Strength (Psalm 46:1)

Lord, as Psalm 46:1 declares, "God is our refuge and strength, an ever-present help in trouble," I seek Your shelter in times of distress and danger. Be my fortress against the adversities of life, and the rock upon which I stand. Your mighty power and unfailing love are the sources of my security. In You, I find protection from the evils that lurk in the darkness and the strength to face them with confidence.

Surround me with Your divine protection and fill my heart with the assurance of Your safeguarding grace. As I walk through the valleys of uncertainty and fear, let Your rod and staff comfort me. Keep me and my loved ones under the shadow of Your wings, where we are safe from all that seeks to harm us. Let Your light guide us through every dark moment, and Your shield protect us from the arrows of the enemy.

In Jesus' name, I pray

Amen.

Prayer 6: The Armor of God" (Ephesians 6:11)

Merciful Savior, guided by Ephesians 6:11, "Put on the full armor of God, so that you can take your stand against the devil's schemes," I seek to arm myself with Your spiritual armor. Grant me the belt of truth, the breastplate of righteousness, and the shield of faith to defend against the deceptions and temptations of evil. May the helmet of salvation guard my thoughts, and the sword of the Spirit, which is Your word, be my defense and guide.

In the spiritual battles I face, remind me that the victory is already won through Your sacrifice and resurrection. Help me to stand firm in faith, clothed in the armor of Your making, resilient in the face of evil's advances. May my feet be fitted with the readiness that comes from the gospel of peace, enabling me to spread Your word and walk confidently in the assurance of Your protection and love.

In Jesus' name, I pray

Amen.

Prayer 7: Guarded by Divine Strength (2 Thessalonians 3:3)

Heavenly Father, in alignment with 2 Thessalonians 3:3, "But the Lord is faithful, and he will strengthen you and protect you from the evil one," I seek Your powerful protection in my life. You are my steadfast guardian against all forms of evil. In Your divine strength, I find the courage and fortitude to face the challenges and temptations of the world. Shield me, Lord, from the deceptive snares laid by the enemy, and fortify my spirit against the tides of darkness that threaten to overwhelm.

I pray for Your encompassing shield to be around me and my loved ones. Your faithfulness is my fortress, and in You, I place my unwavering trust. Guard my heart and mind from the influences that seek to corrupt and lead astray. In the face of adversity, let Your Word be my guide and Your wisdom my path to righteousness. Let me dwell under the safety of Your wing, confident in Your promise of protection and deliverance.

In the moments of doubt and fear, I turn to You, my rock and my redeemer. Strengthen me with Your might, and let Your presence be a constant reassurance in my life. May I walk each day under the banner of Your love, secure in the knowledge that no force of evil can prevail against Your sovereign power.

In Jesus' name, I pray

Amen.

Prayer 8: The Shield of Faith (Ephesians 6:16)

Lord, as Ephesians 6:16 says, "In addition to all this, take up the shield of faith, with which you can extinguish all the flaming arrows of the evil one," I lift up my shield of faith, trusting in Your protection and power. In a world where evil manifests in many forms, I cling to the faith that anchors me in Your truth and love. Help me to stand firm in belief, unwavering in the face of the enemy's tactics, and confident in Your ultimate victory over all that seeks to harm.

I ask for the discernment to recognize the works of darkness and the resilience to resist them. Let my faith be a protective barrier, extinguishing the doubts and fears that the enemy hurls my way. Strengthen my resolve to follow Your ways and to live out Your commandments, even when the path is fraught with challenges. May my life be a testament to the power of faith in overcoming evil, and a beacon of hope to others who face similar trials.

In this spiritual warfare, I lean not on my understanding but on Your omnipotence. Equip me with the full armor of God, that I may be prepared for every battle and stand victorious in Your might. Let my faith in You be unshakeable, a shining light that guides my steps and dispels the darkness around me.

In Jesus' name, I pray,

Amen.

Prayer 9: Safe in His Hands (John 10:28-29)

Merciful Savior, inspired by John 10:28-29, "I give them eternal life, and they shall never perish; no one will snatch them out of my hand," I rest in the assurance of Your protection and care. In a world filled with uncertainty and malice, I find solace in knowing that I am held securely in Your hands. You are my refuge and strength, a constant presence that shields me from the dangers that lurk in the shadows.

I pray for Your guarding hand over my life and the lives of those I love. Keep us safe from the influences that seek to lead us away from Your path. In every decision, guide us with Your wisdom, and in every challenge, strengthen us with Your might. Your love is a fortress that shelters us from the storm, and in Your embrace, we find the courage to face each day.

As I navigate through the trials and tribulations of life, let me always be aware of Your encompassing protection. Remind me that nothing can separate me from Your love and that in You, I find an unassailable sanctuary. May I live each day with a heart full of gratitude for Your constant care, walking boldly in the light of Your protection and grace.

In Jesus' name, I pray, Amen.

Prayer 10: Shelter in the Storm (Psalm 91:1-2)

Heavenly Father, as expressed in Psalm 91:1-2, "Whoever dwells in the shelter of the Most High will rest in the shadow of the Almighty. I will say of the Lord, He is my refuge and my fortress, my God, in whom I trust," I seek Your divine protection. In a world where evil and uncertainty abound, be my safe haven, my shelter from the storm. Let Your presence envelop me, shielding me from harm and guiding me through every challenge.

I pray for Your watchful eye to guard not only me but also my loved ones from the snares of the enemy. In moments of vulnerability, be our strength and fortress. May Your wisdom guide our paths away from deception and danger, leading us to walk in the light of Your truth and love. Surround us with Your angels, ensuring our steps are firm and our spirits undeterred by the darkness around us.

In the face of adversity, remind us of Your unyielding protection and unfailing love. Strengthen our faith and resolve, so that we may stand firm in the truth of Your Word. May the shield of Your faithfulness deflect every negative influence and attack, keeping us safe under the canopy of Your care.

In Jesus' name, I pray, Amen.

Prayer 11: Guarded by His Grace (2 Thessalonians 3:3)

Lord, in alignment with 2 Thessalonians 3:3, "But the Lord is faithful, and he will strengthen you and protect you from the evil one," I place my trust in Your unwavering protection. In these times of trial and temptation, fortify me with Your strength. Let Your grace be the barrier that shields me from the wiles of the evil one. As I navigate through life's uncertainties, keep me anchored in Your righteousness, resilient against the tides of malevolence.

I ask for Your vigilant protection over my thoughts and actions. Guide me in discernment, that I may recognize and resist the temptations and deceptions of the enemy. Infuse my heart with Your courage and my mind with Your wisdom, so that I may make choices that honor You. Let Your Holy Spirit be my constant companion, advising and directing me in the way I should go.

In every situation, may I feel the assurance of Your protective embrace. Shield my family and me from the negative influences that seek to disrupt our peace and harmony. Let us be a testament to Your protective grace, living examples of Your love and strength in a world that often feels overwhelming and chaotic.

In Jesus' name, I pray, Amen.

Prayer 12: The Armor of God (Ephesians 6:10-11)

Merciful Savior, guided by Ephesians 6:10-11, "Finally, be strong in the Lord and in his mighty power. Put on the full armor of God, so that you can take your stand against the devil's schemes," I seek to arm myself with Your spiritual protection. In the battles against spiritual wickedness, let me be clad in the armor of God - the belt of truth, the breastplate of righteousness, the gospel of peace, the shield of faith, the helmet of salvation, and the sword of the Spirit, which is Your Word.

Grant me the wisdom to use this armor effectively, standing firm in faith and truth. May I wield the sword of the Spirit with skill, using Your Word to combat the lies and deceits of the enemy. Let the shield of faith quench all the fiery darts of the wicked, and the helmet of salvation protect my thoughts from despair and doubt. In the breastplate of righteousness, safeguard my heart from the temptations that assail it.

In this spiritual warfare, remind me that the battle belongs to You, Lord. May I find my strength not in my abilities but in Your mighty power. Equip me for each day's challenges, ensuring that I am always prepared to face the forces of darkness with the light of Your truth shining brightly in and through me.

In Jesus' name, I pray,

Amen.

Personal notes:

_____

_____

_____

_____

_____

_____

_____

_____

_____

_____

_____

_____

_____

_____

_____

_____

Prayers for Spiritual Healing

Healing prayers are powerful as they seek God's divine intervention to restore health and bring comfort in times of illness or suffering. In **James 5:15**, the Bible says, "***And the prayer offered in faith will make the sick person well; the Lord will raise them up. If they have sinned, they will be forgiven.***" This verse emphasizes the healing power of prayer and faith in God's ability to heal. By praying for healing, you express trust in God's mercy and power, inviting His presence to bring physical, emotional, and spiritual restoration

Prayer 1: He Restores My Soul (Psalm 23:3)

Heavenly Father, in the spirit of Psalm 23:3, "He restores my soul," I come before You seeking spiritual healing and renewal. In the midst of life's turmoil and challenges, my soul yearns for Your restorative touch. Renew my spirit, Lord, and fill me with Your peace. Wash away the weariness and pain that burden my heart, and replace them with Your joy and strength.

I pray for the healing of emotional wounds and the mending of brokenness within me. Let Your love penetrate the deepest parts of my being, bringing healing where there has been hurt and wholeness where there has been fragmentation. In You, I find refuge and hope. May Your grace work within me, healing and renewing, so that I may reflect Your love and light to others.

In Jesus' name, I pray,

Amen.

Prayer 2: By His Wounds We are Healed (Isaiah 53:5)

Lord, as Isaiah 53:5 declares, "But he was pierced for our transgressions, he was crushed for our iniquities; the punishment that brought us peace was on him, and by his wounds we are healed," I seek Your healing for my spirit. In the sacrifice of Jesus, I find the hope and means for my own spiritual restoration. Heal the wounds of my past, the scars of sin and regret, and let Your grace wash over me, creating a pure heart within.

I ask for Your healing power to touch every aspect of my spiritual life. Strengthen my faith where it is weak, ignite my passion where it has dimmed, and restore the joy of my salvation. In Your mercy, Lord, renew my spirit, so that I may walk in freedom and light, carrying the hope and peace that comes from Your healing love.

In Jesus' name, I pray, Amen.

Prayer 3: Renewed in His Love (Ephesians 4:23-24)

Merciful Savior, inspired by Ephesians 4:23-24, "to be made new in the attitude of your minds; and to put on the new self, created to be like God in true righteousness and holiness," I seek spiritual rejuvenation. In the trials and tribulations of life, let my spirit be refreshed and renewed by Your love. Transform my mind, that I may embrace a new perspective, one rooted in Your truth and grace.

I pray for the revitalization of my faith and the deepening of my relationship with You. Let my spirit be aligned with Yours, filled with Your wisdom and understanding. In Your love, let me find the strength to overcome challenges and the grace to grow in spiritual maturity. Renew me from the inside out, Lord, so that my life may be a testimony to Your transforming power.

In Jesus' name, I pray, Amen.

Prayer 4: Waves of Renewal (Lamentations 3:22-23)

Heavenly Father, as Your mercies are new every morning, as declared in Lamentations 3:22-23, I come before You seeking spiritual healing and renewal. In a world that often feels overwhelming, Your steadfast love and endless mercy are my source of hope and strength. Wash over me with Your waves of renewal, cleansing my spirit of despair and filling me with Your peace.

I ask for the restoration of my soul, that I may find solace in Your presence and rejuvenation in Your love. Heal the wounds that life has inflicted, the unseen scars that hinder my spiritual growth. Guide me through the process of healing, teaching me to lay down my burdens at Your feet and to find rest in the assurance of Your care.

Empower me to rise each day with renewed faith and a heart open to Your transformative grace. Let my spirit soar on the wings of Your love, finding freedom from past hurts and the courage to embrace the journey ahead. May my life reflect the beauty of Your healing power, serving as a testament to Your compassion and faithfulness.

In Jesus' name, I pray, Amen.

Prayer 5: The Path to Wholeness (Psalm 147:3)

Lord, You promise in Psalm 147:3 to heal the brokenhearted and bind up their wounds. In seeking Your face for spiritual healing, I trust in Your ability to mend what is broken within me. Your understanding is infinite, and Your capacity to heal knows no bounds. Reach into the depths of my heart, Lord, and begin the delicate work of healing, knitting together the pieces that have been torn apart by life's trials.

Grant me the courage to face the pain that comes with healing, knowing that You are with me every step of the way. Provide me with the strength to let go of past hurts, to forgive those who have wronged me, and to accept Your forgiveness for my failings. In Your mercy, restore my spirit, making it whole and vibrant, reflective of Your love and grace.

As You work within me, creating a masterpiece from my brokenness, may my journey of healing inspire others who are struggling. Let my life be a beacon of hope, a living example of Your restorative power. Through the valleys and the mountaintops, keep me anchored in Your love, walking the path to wholeness with confidence in Your faithful companionship.

In Jesus' name, I pray, Amen.

Prayer 6: Light in the Darkness (John 8:12)

Merciful Savior, You declare in John 8:12, "I am the light of the world. Whoever follows me will never walk in darkness, but will have the light of life." In this moment of prayer for spiritual healing, I seek Your illuminating presence to dispel the shadows that cloud my spirit. Shine Your light upon me, Lord, revealing the areas in need of Your healing touch and guiding me toward wholeness.

Illuminate the path of healing with Your wisdom and truth, helping me to navigate through the challenges that hinder my spiritual well-being. Let Your light penetrate the deepest recesses of my heart, driving out fear, doubt, and despair. In their place, instill hope, faith, and love, so that I may walk in the assurance of Your light, free from the bondage of past afflictions.

May Your radiant presence be a constant source of comfort and strength as I journey toward healing. In Your light, let me find the clarity and peace that come from a deep, abiding relationship with You. Transform my trials into testimonies of Your grace, that I may shine brightly in this world, reflecting the light of Your love and the hope of Your healing.

In Jesus' name, I pray, Amen.

Prayer 7: Mending the Brokenhearted (Psalm 147:3)

Heavenly Father, as Psalm 147:3 promises, "He heals the brokenhearted and binds up their wounds," I come to You with a heart aching from loss and betrayal. In Your boundless compassion, please touch my wounded heart with Your healing hands. Mend what has been shattered, and soothe the pain that throbs with every beat. Let Your love and grace be the balm that restores my spirit, making me whole once more.

I pray for strength to move beyond the hurt, to forgive those who have caused this pain, and to release the burden of bitterness. Guide me in the path of healing, leading me from darkness into Your glorious light. May I find solace in Your presence, comfort in Your promises, and the courage to open my heart again to the beauty of life and love.

In Jesus' name, I pray, Amen.

Prayer 8: Renewed Heart, Renewed Hope (Isaiah 40:31)

Lord, inspired by Isaiah 40:31, "But those who hope in the Lord will renew their strength," I seek Your divine renewal for my heartbroken state. In the midst of despair, remind me that hope in You never disappoints. Renew my heart, O Lord, lifting me on the wings of eagles, so I may soar above the trials that weigh me down. Replace my sorrow with joy, my weariness with strength, and my despair with hope.

Empower me to face each day with a renewed sense of purpose and peace. Help me to see the opportunities for growth in this season of healing. May Your unwavering love be the foundation on which I rebuild my life, trusting that Your plans for me are filled with hope and a future. Let me embrace the journey ahead, knowing You walk beside me every step of the way.

In Jesus' name, I pray, Amen.

Prayer 9: From Shadows to Light (Psalm 34:18)

Merciful Savior, Psalm 34:18 assures us, "The Lord is close to the brokenhearted and saves those who are crushed in spirit." In my moments of deepest heartache, I cling to this promise. Be near me now, Lord, as I navigate through the shadows of grief and loss. Shine Your light on my path, guiding me towards healing and wholeness. Let Your presence dispel the darkness, bringing hope to my weary soul.

Grant me the grace to let go of the past, to forgive, and to heal from the inside out. May I learn from my experiences, growing stronger and more compassionate. Transform my pain into purpose, using it to draw me closer to You and to others who suffer. With Your guidance, may I step into the light of a new beginning, filled with Your peace and love.

In Jesus' name, I pray, Amen.

Prayer 10: Healing Streams of Comfort (Psalm 23:2)

Heavenly Father, in the spirit of Psalm 23:2, "He makes me lie down in green pastures, he leads me beside quiet waters," I come before You with a heart heavy with grief and sorrow. In this moment of heartbreak, I seek the comfort of Your presence, the healing streams of Your love that restore the soul. Guide me to the quiet waters of Your peace, where I can find rest and solace in the midst of my turmoil.

I pray for Your healing touch to mend the broken pieces of my heart. Let Your grace wash over me, cleansing me of the pain and filling me with new hope and strength. In the green pastures of Your love, rejuvenate my spirit, allowing me to rise from this place of sorrow with a renewed sense of purpose and joy.

Grant me the courage to walk through this valley of shadows with faith and not fear. Remind me that You are with me every step of the way, Your rod and Your staff comforting me. May this journey of healing draw me closer to You, deepening my trust and reliance on Your unfailing love.

In Jesus' name, I pray

Amen.

Prayer 11: From Mourning to Dancing (Psalm 30:11)

Lord, as declared in Psalm 30:11, "You turned my mourning into dancing; you removed my sackcloth and clothed me with joy," I stand in need of Your transformative power. This heartache feels overwhelming, yet I believe in Your promise to turn my sorrow into joy. Lift the weight of sadness from my shoulders and replace it with the garment of praise, that I may dance in the light of Your love.

I ask for Your comfort and strength in this time of loss. Help me to navigate the complex emotions of grief, guiding me gently towards acceptance and peace. In Your mercy, heal the wounds of my heart, and restore my spirit with the hope and brightness of Your presence.

May this season of healing become a testament to Your grace and compassion. Transform my pain into a deeper understanding of Your love and a greater capacity to love others. Let my life reflect the beauty of Your redemption, shining brightly as a beacon of hope to those who also walk through seasons of sorrow.

In Jesus' name, I pray, Amen.

Prayer 12: The Light of Hope (2 Corinthians 4:6)

Merciful Savior, inspired by 2 Corinthians 4:6, "For God, who said, 'Let light shine out of darkness, 'made his light shine in our hearts to give us the light of the knowledge of God's glory displayed in the face of Christ," I come to You amidst the shadows of heartbreak, seeking the light of Your hope. Illuminate my path with the brilliance of Your love, guiding me out of despair and into the warmth of Your presence.

In this time of healing, let Your light penetrate the darkest corners of my heart, revealing Your promises of comfort and renewal. Strengthen my faith, that I may see beyond the pain to the promise of a new day dawning, filled with the joy and peace that only YOou can provide.

Help me to cling to the hope that is found in You, the assurance that no matter how deep the hurt, Your love is deeper still. May this process of healing not only restore my heart but also transform it, making it more resilient, compassionate, and reflective of Your light. In the journey from heartbreak to healing, let me be a witness to Your enduring faithfulness and love.

In Jesus' name, I pray

Amen.

Special Prayers

Prayer for Discernment

Prayers 1: Gift of Discernment
(Philippians 1:9-10)

Heavenly Father, as Paul prayed in Philippians 1:9-10, "And this is my prayer: that your love may abound more and more in knowledge and depth of insight, so that you may be able to discern what is best and may be pure and blameless for the day of Christ," I too seek the gift of discernment. In a world filled with myriad voices and choices, grant me the wisdom to discern Your will, to distinguish between the paths that lead to life and those that lead away from You. Illuminate my mind and heart, that I might navigate life's complexities with clarity and make decisions that honor You.

Strengthen my understanding and deepen my love for Your truth, that my discernment may be rooted in a desire to faithfully follow You. Help me to see beyond the surface, to judge not by appearances but with righteous judgment as Jesus taught. In every decision, big or small, guide me by Your Spirit, that my actions might reflect

Your love and wisdom, leading me closer to Your heart and Your purposes for my life.

In Jesus' name, I pray, Amen.

Prayer 2: Wisdom's Path" (James 1:5)

Lord, James 1:5 encourages us, "If any of you lacks wisdom, you should ask God, who gives generously to all without finding fault, and it will be given to you." In seeking discernment, I come to You, the fount of all wisdom, asking for the insight and understanding necessary to navigate the challenges and decisions before me. Bestow upon me the wisdom that comes from above, pure, peace-loving, considerate, submissive, full of mercy and good fruit, impartial and sincere. Let this wisdom guide my thoughts, words, and actions.

Equip me with the humility to seek Your guidance in all things, acknowledging that true wisdom and discernment come from You alone. In the face of uncertainty, remind me to turn to You first, to listen for Your voice, and to be guided by Your gentle nudging. May my life be a testament to the wisdom You provide, demonstrating a discerning spirit that seeks to do Your will and glorify Your name in every circumstance.

In Jesus' name, I pray, Amen.

Prayer 3: Clarity of Vision" (Proverbs 3:5-6)

Merciful Savior, Proverbs 3:5-6 instructs, "Trust in the Lord with all your heart and lean not on your own understanding; in all your ways submit to Him, and He will make your paths straight." I seek Your guidance for clarity of vision and discernment. Help me to trust in You wholeheartedly, not relying on my own limited perspective but on Your infinite wisdom. Guide my steps and decisions, that I may walk in the certainty of Your will, confident that You are leading me in the way everlasting.

Teach me to submit my plans and desires to You, knowing that Your plans are higher than mine and Your ways perfect. Open my eyes to see the direction You have for me, and grant me the courage to follow, even when the path seems uncertain. May Your Spirit illuminate the way, providing discernment in every decision and clarity amidst confusion, so that I may live out Your purpose for my life with faith and confidence.

In Jesus' name, I pray

Amen.

Personal notes:

_____

_____

_____

_____

_____

_____

_____

_____

_____

_____

_____

_____

_____

_____

_____

Prayer to Cancel Evil Plan

Prayer 1: No Weapon Formed Shall Prosper (Isaiah 54:17)

Heavenly Father, as declared in Isaiah 54:17, "No weapon forged against you will prevail, and you will refute every tongue that accuses you," I stand in the assurance of Your protection against every evil plan. I come before You today to seek Your divine intervention, to cancel and nullify every scheme the enemy has plotted against me, my family, and those I hold dear. Surround us with Your shield of protection, ensuring that no harm nor danger comes our way.

I pray for wisdom and discernment to recognize the snares set before us and the strength to stand firm in faith, resisting every form of evil. Let Your truth be our guide, and Your Word our defense, as we navigate through the challenges set against us. May Your peace that surpasses all understanding guard our hearts and minds, keeping us secure in the knowledge that we are more than conquerors through Him who loves us.

In Jesus' name, I pray, Amen.

Prayer 2: The Lord is My Light and My Salvation" (Psalm 27:1)

Lord, inspired by Psalm 27:1, "The Lord is my light and my salvation–whom shall I fear? The Lord is the stronghold of my life–of whom shall I be afraid?" I call upon Your mighty power to dismantle every evil plan formed against me. Illuminate the darkness with Your light, revealing hidden dangers and providing a path of escape from the enemy's designs. Be my fortress and my safe haven, where no evil can withstand Your presence.

Grant me courage and boldness to face the adversities with confidence, knowing You are by my side. Strengthen my faith to believe in Your promise of deliverance and victory over every form of wickedness. As I place my trust in You, let me witness the downfall of every plot meant to cause distress or harm, affirming that my security and victory are found in You alone.

In Jesus' name, I pray

Amen.

Prayer 3: Delivered from the Snare" (2 Timothy 4:18)

Merciful Savior, echoing the words of 2 Timothy 4:18, "The Lord will rescue me from every evil attack and will bring me safely to his heavenly kingdom," I seek Your mighty hand to protect and deliver me from the clutches of the enemy. Break every chain of evil intent, and set me free from the plans devised to entrap me. Let Your angelic forces be dispatched to shield me, creating a barrier through which no evil can penetrate.

I ask for the anointing of the Holy Spirit to empower me with authority over every demonic scheme. Let every plan of darkness be exposed to the light of Your truth, rendering it powerless. May I walk in the liberty and freedom You have won for me, proclaiming Your goodness and mercy all the days of my life. Establish my steps in Your Word, and let not the wickedness of this world overcome me.

In Jesus' name, I pray

Amen.

Personal notes:

_____

_____

_____

_____

_____

_____

_____

_____

_____

_____

_____

_____

_____

_____

_____

_____

_____

_____

Prayer to Uncover the Enemy plan

Prayer 1: Light Upon the Shadows (Luke 8:17)

Heavenly Father, as Luke 8:17 tells us, "For there is nothing hidden that will not be disclosed, and nothing concealed that will not be known or brought out into the open," I seek Your divine illumination to uncover the enemy's plans. In a world where darkness seeks to hide its schemes, shine Your light of truth and wisdom upon my path. Reveal the snares and traps set before me and my loved ones, that we may walk in safety, guarded by Your providence.

Grant me the discernment to see beyond the façade, to understand the deeper motives at play. Help me to stand firm in Your strength, equipped with the full armor of God, that I may resist and overcome the wiles of the adversary. May Your guiding light expose every shadow, turning plots of deception into testimonies of Your protection and grace.

In Jesus' name, I pray, Amen.

Prayer 2: The Walls of Jericho Fall (Joshua 6:20)

Lord, just as the walls of Jericho fell at the sound of the Israelites' trumpets in Joshua 6:20, I pray for the downfall of any barriers the enemy has constructed to hinder Your purposes in my life. Break down the fortifications of deceit, the strongholds of fear, and the barriers of confusion that seek to separate me from Your will. Let the truth of Your Word act as a trumpet call, demolishing obstacles and clearing the way for Your light to penetrate the darkest corners of my circumstances.

Empower me with bold faith to march around my Jericho, trusting in Your promise of victory. As the walls come tumbling down, let every concealed plan of the enemy be laid bare, defeated by the power of Your might. In the rubble of these fallen barriers, let me find the stepping stones to deeper faith and closer communion with You, celebrating the triumph of Your righteousness over every enemy scheme.

In Jesus' name, I pray

Amen.

Prayer 3: Unveiled Strategies (Ephesians 5:13)

Merciful Savior, Ephesians 5:13 assures us, "But everything exposed by the light becomes visible–and everything that is illuminated becomes a light." I call upon Your radiant light to expose and nullify the strategies devised against me by the enemy. Illuminate my understanding, that I may see with clarity the tactics meant to derail me from Your path. Transform me into a beacon of Your truth, repelling darkness and spreading light wherever there is shadow.

Provide me with wisdom to navigate through the enemy's illusions, recognizing falsehoods and standing confidently in Your promises. Strengthen my resolve to follow Your lead, allowing no plan of darkness to take root or flourish. As You unveil the enemy's strategies, equip me to counter them with Your Word, ensuring that in every battle, Your light triumphs over darkness, and Your purposes prevail in my life.

In Jesus' name, I pray

Amen.

Personal notes:

_____

_____

_____

_____

_____

_____

_____

_____

_____

_____

_____

_____

_____

_____

_____

_____

_____

Prayer to Reveal Hidden Things

Prayer 1: Illuminate the Hidden (Luke 8:17)

Heavenly Father, as proclaimed in Luke 8:17, "For there is nothing hidden that will not be disclosed, nor is anything secret that will not become known and come to light," I stand before You seeking the illumination of Your truth in my life. In the complexities and the challenges that I face, there are things concealed from my understanding. I pray for Your light to shine upon these hidden matters, revealing the truth that lies beneath, guiding me to make decisions that align with Your will and purpose for my life.

Empower me with Your Holy Spirit to discern the revelations You provide, to act wisely upon them, and to remain steadfast in Your path. May the unveiling of these secrets not only bring clarity to my journey but also strengthen my faith and trust in You. Let me embrace the knowledge You reveal with a heart ready to follow Your lead, transforming my life and those around me for Your glory.

In Jesus' name, I pray

Amen.

Prayer 2: Secrets Unfolded (Jeremiah 33:3)

Lord Almighty, inspired by Jeremiah 33:3, "Call to me and I will answer you and tell you great and unsearchable things you do not know," I reach out to You with a heart full of questions and a mind seeking understanding. In my life, there are puzzles and challenges that seem insurmountable, and I look to You for the wisdom and insight needed to uncover the answers. I ask that You reveal the secrets that are beyond my comprehension, showing me the path through the trials and the mysteries that cloud my vision.

Strengthen my heart to receive Your revelations with grace and courage. As You unfold the secrets of Your kingdom and the plans You have for me, help me to walk in obedience and faithfulness, trusting that Your ways are higher than my ways. Let the knowledge of these hidden things be a source of strength and hope, guiding me closer to You and the destiny You have ordained for me.

In Jesus' name, I pray,

Amen.

Prayer 3: Pathways of Truth Revealed (Psalm 119:130)

Gracious God, echoing Psalm 119:130, "The unfolding of Your words gives light; it gives understanding to the simple," I seek Your guidance to unveil the paths and truths hidden from my sight. In a world filled with confusion and deception, Your Word is the beacon that pierces the darkness, revealing the way forward. I ask for the unfolding of Your wisdom in my life, that each step I take may be grounded in Your truth, leading me towards the fulfillment of Your promises and the realization of my God-given purpose.

May the revelation of Your Word enlighten my understanding, and the insight gained from Your truths equip me to face life's challenges with confidence and peace. Help me to apply the knowledge revealed to me in ways that honor You and reflect Your love to those I encounter. In the discovery of Your hidden truths, let my life be a testament to Your faithfulness and a witness to the transforming power of Your light.

In Jesus' name, I pray

Amen.

Personal notes:

_____

_____

_____

_____

_____

_____

_____

_____

_____

_____

_____

_____

Prayer to Protect your Home

Prayer 1: A Shield Around My Home (Psalm 3:3)

Heavenly Father, as Psalm 3:3 declares, "But you, Lord, are a shield around me," I pray for Your divine protection to encompass my home and all who dwell within. Let Your presence be a fortress that guards us against the assaults of the enemy and the dangers of this world. May Your shield of protection deflect any harm or negativity that tries to enter our sanctuary, keeping us safe under the shadow of Your wings.

Strengthen our household with Your love and peace, ensuring that our foundation is built upon Your unshakeable truths. Bless our coming and going, and watch over us whether we are awake or asleep. May our home be a place of refuge and a testament to Your grace, where Your spirit dwells richly, guiding us in unity and love.

In Jesus' name, I pray, Amen.

Prayer 2: Guardian of Our Dwelling (Proverbs 2:8)

Lord, inspired by Proverbs 2:8, "for he guards the course of the just and protects the way of his faithful ones," I ask You to be the guardian of our dwelling. Surround our home with Your vigilant care, ensuring that every corner is under Your watchful eye. Protect us from the snares and temptations that seek to invade our peace, and let Your wisdom be our guide in every decision we make within these walls.

Let our home be a beacon of Your love and hope, a place where Your teachings are lived out daily. Fill it with Your presence, Lord, so that all who enter may feel Your peace and know Your love. May our dwelling be a sanctuary of faith, where we grow closer to You and to each other, shielded by Your providential care.

In Jesus' name, I pray, Amen.

Prayer 3: Foundation of Peace (Isaiah 32:18)

Merciful Savior, echoing Isaiah 32:18, "My people will live in peaceful dwelling places, in secure homes, in undisturbed places of rest," I pray for Your peace to reign within our home. Make it a place of serenity and security, where fear has no hold, and Your tranquility soothes our hearts. May our residence be a testament to Your promise of peace, a secure haven where Your blessings flow abundantly.

Grant us the wisdom to create a home that reflects Your love, nurturing an environment where Your Word flourishes and Your peace prevails. Protect us from the conflicts and challenges that may arise, wrapping our home in the assurance of Your protection and care. May our family bonds be strengthened, and our faith deepened, as we live out Your peace in our daily interactions and decisions.

In Jesus' name, I pray

Amen.

Personal notes:

_____

_____

_____

_____

_____

_____

_____

_____

_____

_____

_____

_____

_____

_____

_____

_____

Prayer to Reveal the Truth

Prayer 1: Light of Truth (John 8:32)

Heavenly Father, inspired by the words of John 8:32, "Then you will know the truth, and the truth will set you free," I seek Your illumination in areas of my life shrouded in uncertainty and deception. Illuminate my path with the light of Your truth, revealing what has been hidden and clarifying what has been murky. Let Your Word be a lamp unto my feet, guiding me in the way of wisdom and integrity, and exposing the falsehoods that seek to ensnare me.

Grant me the discernment to recognize Your truth amidst the clamor of the world's voices. Strengthen my resolve to follow Your ways, even when faced with challenges and opposition. May the revelation of truth bring liberation and peace, freeing me from the chains of confusion and doubt, and leading me into a deeper relationship with You, grounded in trust and faithfulness.

In Jesus' name, I pray

Amen.

Prayer 2: Unveil What is Hidden (Luke 12:2)

Lord, echoing the assurance found in Luke 12:2, "There is nothing concealed that will not be disclosed, or hidden that will not be made known," I come before You asking for the unveiling of truths in my life and the situations I am facing. Reveal the motives and intentions behind the actions of those around me, and uncover any hidden agendas that may affect my wellbeing and spiritual growth. Let nothing remain hidden that could hinder my walk with You or the fulfillment of Your plans for my life.

Equip me with the wisdom to navigate the truths You reveal, using them to make informed decisions and to act in alignment with Your will. Help me to approach what You unveil with a spirit of love and forgiveness, seeking reconciliation where there is division and understanding where there is conflict. May the truth serve not as a weapon, but as a bridge to deeper connections and healing, both with You and those in my life.

In Jesus' name, I pray

Amen.

Prayer 3: Wisdom's Revelation (James 1:5)

Merciful Savior, as James 1:5 promises, "If any of you lacks wisdom, you should ask God, who gives generously to all without finding fault, and it will be given to you," I call upon Your boundless generosity to grant me the wisdom needed to discern truth from falsehood. In a world rife with half-truths and outright lies, provide me with the clarity of thought and purity of heart to see through the deception, to understand Your will, and to live by the principles of Your kingdom.

Encourage my heart to seek Your wisdom diligently, trusting that You will reveal what I need to know in Your perfect timing. Let this quest for truth and wisdom draw me closer to You, shaping my character and guiding my actions. May the truth You reveal inspire me to walk in righteousness, leading by example and shining Your light into the lives of others, dispelling darkness and spreading hope.

In Jesus' name, I pray

Amen.

Personal notes:

_____

_____

_____

_____

_____

_____

_____

_____

_____

_____

_____

_____

_____

_____

_____

_____

Prayer to Ask God to forgive your Sin

Prayer 1: A Heart Renewed (Psalm 51:10)

Heavenly Father, in the spirit of David's plea in Psalm 51:10, "Create in me a pure heart, O God, and renew a steadfast spirit within me," I come before You acknowledging my shortcomings and the sins that have distanced me from You. I ask for Your forgiveness, for the times I've wandered from Your path and allowed my weaknesses to lead me astray. Wash me clean of my transgressions, and let Your grace restore the joy of Your salvation in my heart.

Teach me, Lord, to hold fast to Your ways, learning from my mistakes and growing in Your wisdom. May this moment of repentance be a turning point, leading me to a deeper understanding of Your love and mercy. Help me to live each day with a renewed spirit, committed to walking in righteousness and reflecting Your love to those around me.

In Jesus' name, I pray, Amen.

Prayer 2: Forgiveness Flows (1 John 1:9)

Lord, I cling to the promise of 1 John 1:9, "If we confess our sins, He is faithful and just and will forgive us our sins and purify us from all unrighteousness." I confess to You now the ways in which I have failed to live up to Your holy standards, the moments of weakness, and the choices that have led me away from You. In Your mercy, forgive me, cleanse me, and guide me back to the path of righteousness.

I am grateful for Your unfailing love and Your willingness to forgive time and again. Strengthen me with Your Holy Spirit, that I may resist temptation and live in a way that honors You. Let Your forgiveness transforms my heart, leading me to forgive others as You have forgiven me, and spreading Your grace and love in every aspect of my life.

In Jesus' name, I pray, Amen.